# Principles of Economics

# Principles of Economics

Richard W. Tresch

BOSTON COLLEGE

WEST PUBLISHING COMPANY

Minneapolis/Saint Paul    New York    Los Angeles    San Francisco

## PRODUCTION CREDITS

COPYEDITING Sherry Goldbecker
TEXT DESIGN Kristin Weber
TEXT ILLUSTRATIONS Randy Miyake, Miyake Illustration
PAGE LAYOUT David Farr, ImageSmythe, Inc.
COMPOSITION Parkwood Composition
INDEX E. Virginia Hobbs
COVER DESIGN David Farr, ImageSmythe, Inc.
PART-CHAPTER OPENING ART/COVER IMAGE Maxine Masterfield, AWS, NWS, from *In Harmony with Nature*, by Maxine Masterfield, published by Watson Guptill, New York

Production, Prepress, Printing, and Binding by West Publishing Company.

Chapter 41 of this text was written by Jonathan Wight, University of Richmond.

## WEST'S COMMITMENT TO THE ENVIRONMENT

In 1906, West Publishing Company began recycling materials left over from the production of books. This began a tradition of efficient and responsible use of resources. Today, up to 95 percent of our legal books and 70 percent of our college and school texts are printed on recycled, acid-free stock. West also recycles nearly 22 million pounds of scrap paper annually—the equivalent of 181,717 trees. Since the 1960s, West has devised ways to capture and recycle waste inks, solvents, oils, and vapors created in the printing process. We also recycle plastics of all kinds, wood, glass, corrugated cardboard, and batteries, and have eliminated the use of Styrofoam book packaging. We at West are proud of the longevity and the scope of our commitment to the environment.

Printed in the United States of America

01 00 99 98 97 96 95 94 8 7 6 5 4 3 2 1 0

**Library of Congress Cataloging-in-Publication Data**

Tresch, Richard W.
Principles of economics / Richard Tresch.
p. cm.
Includes index
ISBN 0-314-02754-8
1. Economics. I. Title.
HB171.5.T654 1994
330—dc20

93-5948
CIP

*With love to*
*Alayne, Kimberly, Sara*
*and*
*my parents*

*and with special thanks to*
*Ken Felter*

# CONTENTS IN BRIEF

# TABLE OF CONTENTS

## PART I
## INTRODUCTION 1

### CHAPTER 1
### THE FIRST PRINCIPLES OF ECONOMICS 3



### CHAPTER 2
### SOLVING THE ECONOMIC PROBLEM 17



### CHAPTER 3
### SOCIETY'S ECONOMIC PROBLEM 37



### CHAPTER 4
### MARKET, PRICES, AND THE U.S. ECONOMY 69

PART II

## THE LAWS OF SUPPLY AND DEMAND 97

CHAPTER 5

## DEMAND AND ELASTICITY 99



CHAPTER 6

## SUPPLY AND MARGINAL COST 127



CHAPTER 7

## MARKET EQUILIBRIUM: THE LAWS OF SUPPLY AND DEMAND 155



CHAPTER 8

## APPLICATIONS OF SUPPLY AND DEMAND 181

CHAPTER 11

## THE FIRM'S HOW PROBLEM AND THE TOTAL COST OF PRODUCTION 277



CHAPTER 12

## PRIVATE INVESTMENT ANALYSIS 311



APPENDIX 12

## Cost Benefit Analysis 329



PART IV

# THE STRUCTURE OF PRODUCT MARKETS IN THE UNITED STATES 337



CHAPTER 13

## PERFECT COMPETITITON 345



APPENDIX 13

## The Relationship Between Long-Run and Short-Run Costs 383

CHAPTER 14

## PURE MONOPOLY 389



CHAPTER 15

## SOFTENING COMPETITION: FROM COLLUSION TO EFFECTIVELY COMPETITIVE MARKETS 421



CHAPTER 16

## OLIGOPOLY 445



CHAPTER 17

## PUBLIC POLICY AND THE BIG BUSINESS SECTOR 465

**Key Terms** 497
**Questions** 497
**CASE: Some Skies are Contestable, Others are Not** 498

PART VII

# INTRODUCTION TO MACROECONOMIC THEORY AND POLICY 697

CHAPTER 25

## THE MACROECONOMIC POLICY GOALS I: LONG-RUN ECONOMIC GROWTH AND FULL EMPLOYMENT 699



CHAPTER 26

## THE MACROECONOMIC POLICY GOALS II: PRICE STABILITY AND STABLE INTERNATIONAL ECONOMIC RELATIONS 731



CHAPTER 27

## THE NATIONAL INCOME AND PRODUCT ACCOUNTS 763

CHAPTER 28

## MODELING THE MACRO ECONOMY: NEW CLASSICAL AND NEW KEYNESIAN PERSPECTIVES 795



PART VIII

# NATIONAL INCOME DETERMINATION, FISCAL POLICY, AND UNEMPLOYMENT 827

CHAPTER 29

## NATIONAL INCOME DETERMINATION 829



APPENDIX 29

## Algebraic Analysis of Equilibrium 868



CHAPTER 30

## THE SPENDING MULTIPLIER, FISCAL POLICY, AND UNEMPLOYMENT 873

APPENDIX 30

## Algebra of the Spending Multiplier and the Fiscal Policy Multipliers 910



CHAPTER 31

## AUTOMATIC STABILIZERS, NET EXPORTS, AND BUDGET DEFICITS 915



APPENDIX 31

## Algebraic Analysis of Income Taxes and Net Exports 949



CHAPTER 32

## BUSINESS CYCLES: THE MULTIPLIER-ACCELERATOR MODEL AND THE REAL BUSINESS CYCLE 953



---

PART IX

# MONEY AND MONETARY POLICY 981

CHAPTER 33

## THE NATURE OF MONEY AND BANKING: FIRST PRINCIPLES 983

CHAPTER 34

## THE MONETARY SYSTEM OF THE UNITED STATES 1009



APPENDIX 34

## The Troubled Savings and Loan Industry 1032



CHAPTER 35

## MONETARY POLICY 1037



CHAPTER 36

## FISCAL POLICY, MONETARY POLICY, AND THE MACROECONOMIC POLICY GOALS 1073

PART X

# THE ROLE OF PRICES AND THE PROBLEM OF INFLATION 1103

CHAPTER 37

## AGGREGATE SUPPLY AND AGGREGATE DEMAND 1105



CHAPTER 38

## CONTROLLING INFLATION AND OTHER POLICY ISSUES 1137



PART XI

# INTERNATIONAL ECONOMIC ISSUES 1173

CHAPTER 39

## INTERNATIONAL TRADE AND BARRIERS TO TRADE 1175



CHAPTER 40

## INTERNATIONAL FINANCE 1207

CHAPTER 41

## DEVELOPING NATIONS 1236

# PREFACE

*Principles of Economics* is the product of over twenty years of experience teaching the economic principles course at Boston College. It is a mainstream text that provides in-depth analysis, with examples, of the standard topics in economic principles. Nonetheless, the text contains a number of distinctive content and pedagogical features in both micro and macro that, I believe, distinguish it from other mainstream texts.

## CONTENT FEATURES

### Microeconomics

In my opinion, the fundamental teaching problem in the micro principles course involves teaching our students to view microeconomics as we do. Economists see microeconomics as a unified theory of behavior centered around solving the economic problem (optimization) and the nature of exchange. Our students, in contrast, tend to see the micro course as a set of essentially unrelated topics. I try hard in my own teaching, and in this text, to bring a sense of coherence to the collection of microeconomic principles that we want our students to know.

THE ECONOMIC PROBLEM The chief organizing device is the economic problem itself, with its objectives, alternatives, and constraints. The economic problem serves as a motivating and organizing concept throughout the text, beginning with the four fundamental economic questions in the introduction section and running through demand, supply, the incentives for market exchange, production costs, the behavior of firms in different market structures, and even the entirety of macroeconomics. I begin each new main topic with a discussion of the economic problem that someone is trying to solve.

The focus on the economic problem begins right away in Chapters 1 and 2, which contain a meatier introduction to the economic problem than other texts do. I also present a detailed discussion of the two criteria, efficiency and equity, that economists use to judge the solutions to economic problems. The pursuit of efficiency and equity in turn becomes another organizing and motivating theme throughout the micro (and macro) chapters. For example, the efficiency and equity implications of each product market structure are highlighted and summarized as part of the concluding material in each product market chapter. Surprisingly few texts do this.

WEAVING EXAMPLES INTO THE TEXT Another means I use to promote coherence is to weave examples into the analysis, rather than setting them apart in boxes. Boxed examples tend to disrupt the flow of the exposition, especially when the page also contains a figure and/or a table. I also decided against writing separate chapters on special interest topics such as pollution, energy and natural resources, the economics of information, agriculture, and so forth. Instead I include such topics within the basic micro chapters, where appropriate, as examples illustrating the underlying principles. This approach better serves to reinforce and integrate the basic principles. Nevertheless, the examples involving special interest topics are detailed, enough to cover the basic points that we want our students to know about each topic.

REPETITION OF DATA Finally, I try to build a sense of coherence through the repetition of data. Production data that are used to illustrate marginal product as part of the Law of Diminishing Returns in Chapter 6 reappear in Chapter 9 to illustrate the value of labor's marginal product when developing the demand curve for labor, and reappear again in Chapter 11 to illustrate the connection between marginal product and marginal cost. Cost data presented in Chapter 11 to illustrate long-run and short-run total cost curves are also used for the cost curves in Chapter 13 and 14 on perfect competition and monopoly. The use of common cost data to illustrate perfectly competitive and monopolistic firms helps the student understand the social costs of monopoly power. Ideally, students should see each new topic as an immediate and natural extension of material they have seen before, all contained within a unified structure. The repetition of data helps to this end.

## Additional Features of the Microeconomic Chapters

A BEEFED-UP DISCUSSION OF SUPPLY AND DEMAND EARLY ON The text provides a more detailed, early development of supply and demand that emphasizes both the efficiency properties of competitive markets and why markets form so easily, as well as showing students how competitive markets work. The one or two chapters on supply and demand in many existing texts do a fine job of illustrating how competitive markets operate, but do less well in examining the other two areas. For example, most texts wait until the chapter(s) on perfect competition to demonstrate the efficiency properties of competitive markets. By that time however, students have visions of average and marginal costs curves, not of supply-and-demand curves, dancing in their heads. Teachers of upper-level electives want their students to understand that the supply-and-demand representation of a market indicates the efficient allocation of resources in the market, whatever other purposes those teachers may have in mind when drawing the supply-and-demand diagram.

EARLY ANALYSIS OF LABOR MARKETS The supply-and-demand analysis of labor markets immediately follows the supply-and-demand analysis of product markets, so that students see the similarities between product and factor markets. This is yet another unifying device in the micro chapters. In contrast, in most texts, all factor market analysis appears at the end of the micro section, giving the topic the look and feel of an add-on, to be discussed if time permits.

COST CURVES DEVELOPED AS NEEDED The relevant cost concepts are developed as needed, rather than placed all together in a single blast-of-cost-curves chapter that, in my opinion, is the worst thing writers of economics texts can do to students. My students find traditional cost curve chapters to be totally mechanical, sterile, and void of relevance. I agree with them. Such chapters strike me as displays of an authors' technical virtuosity that provide students with precious little motivation for learning all the cost relationships at that point. Cost relationships themselves cannot be the main point of a chapter that hopes to hold students' interest.

SPECIAL EMPHASIS ON MARGINAL COST Marginal cost, the most important cost concept, appears with the early development of the supply curve in the supply-and-demand chapters, allowing students to become comfortable with marginal cost before confronting the other cost concepts. The marginal cost curve even receives its own color coding throughout the text to keep it highlighted in students' minds. This is part of a strategy to emphasize at every opportunity the importance of the margin to the student. We are bombarded in our everyday lives with averages and totals, yet we hope to teach our students that the margin is what really matters. I believe that presenting the marginal cost curve first is an excellent way to begin. Linking marginal cost to the supply curve right away also allows me to explore, in the supply-and-demand section, the issues of the efficiency of competitive markets and why markets form so easily.

THE TOTAL COST CURVE AND THE FIRM'S HOW PROBLEM Chapter 11 on the costs of production centers around the concept of the total cost curve as the solution to the firm's How problem, offering numerous applications based on a firm's desire to minimize cost. An analysis of industrial air and water pollution appears as one of the applications in this chapter, where I believe it should be. (I hold off on presenting the various average cost curves until Chapter 13 on perfect competition, where they are used to represent profits and losses, and break-even and shutdown points).

OVERVIEW OF THE U.S. ECONOMY An overview of the U.S. economy appears in Chapter 4 of the introductory section, a feature that only some texts provide and that I think is important for students. The introductory section also includes an analysis of the problems and prospects of the Eastern European economies-in-transition, as a means of illustrating the need for societies to choose an economic system.

FLEXIBLE PRESENTATION OF CONSUMER THEORY The text offers a flexible presentation of the theory of the consumer that allows the instructor to choose the intuitive marginal utility explanation or the modern approach, either with or without indifference curves.

FOCUS ON DISTRIBUTIONAL ISSUES The factor market analysis emphasizes distributional issues more than most other texts do, which I know is in line with students' interests.

EMPHASIS ON LABOR MARKET EXPERIENCES OF WOMEN The labor market experience of women in the

United States is one of the leading issues of the day. I describe women's labor market experiences in a number of chapters.

FULL CHAPTER ON PRIVATE INVESTMENT ANALYSIS AND COST-BENEFIT ANALYSIS An entire chapter (Chapter 12) is devoted to private investment analysis, a feature that I believe is unique to this text. Investment analysis is important, and my students have enjoyed this material. The chapter includes a substantial appendix on government cost-benefit analysis.

DETAILED PRESENTATION OF THE FLOW OF FUNDS Chapter 20 on capital markets contains a detailed presentation of the flow of funds through the nation's financial markets. (The flow-of-funds section is also available in the macro split.)

MODERN TREATMENT OF INDUSTRIAL ORGANIZATION Chapters 15–17 contain a thoroughly modern analysis of topics in industrial organization, with emphasis on game theory where appropriate.

INTERNATIONAL PERSPECTIVES ON KEY ISSUES International perspectives on selected key issues appear in sections highlighted by a logo.

## Macroeconomics

The fundamental teaching problem in macroeconomics is rather the opposite of the teaching problem in microeconomics. The problem here is to present the controversy that exists between the new Keynesian and new classical economists over the operation of the macro economy in the short run, and to do so in a way that is fair to both schools yet does not hopelessly confuse our students.

CONTINUED FOCUS ON MACROECONOMIC POLICY GOALS I attempt to confront this fundamental difficulty by tightly structuring the macro chapters around the four macroeconomic policy goals—long-run economic growth, full employment, price stability, and stability in economic relations with foreign nations. The macro chapters begin with an extended discussion of the four macroeconomic policy goals, after which I ask the central policy question of the course: to what extent can the national government's fiscal and monetary policies help to achieve these goals? The government's policy problem is discussed repeatedly throughout the macro chapters, with hypothetical exercises and real-world examples showing what the government is trying to do. The analysis of the controversy between the two schools remains focused on this question throughout.

BALANCED PRESENTATION OF THE NEW KEYNESIAN AND NEW CLASSICAL VIEWS I strive for a balanced presentation of the new Keynesian and new classical views of the macro economy, stressing areas of agreement and disagreement between the two schools. In my opinion, this requires an approach different from the one found in most existing texts. The standard story that students are told as economics texts move early on into the Keynesian cross is that the Keynesian consumption function is a major building block of the demand side of a broader macro model, a model on which macro economists generally agree. In my view, this story is not just a matter of some innocent hand-waving that might be appropriate for a principles course. I think the story is wrong. The real business cycle model is now the prevailing model within the new classical school. In that model, any short-run output response to, say, a productivity shock is to be found in the supply of labor, not in the Keynesian consumption function.

In my opinion, a balanced presentation of the two schools requires three things: which I provide:

a. A more detailed explanation of the Life Cycle Hypothesis than the paragraph or box to which it is relegated in most texts (if it is mentioned at all). The LCH, not the Keynesian consumption function, is the main component of the demand side of the real business cycle model.
b. An analysis of the market for labor from the new classical perspective including, most importantly, the relationship between interest rates and the supply of labor.
c. A comparison of the data that convinces new Keynesian economists that product and factor markets are riddled with imperfections, and the data that convinces new classical economists that the economy is essentially competitive and ought to be modeled as such.

The first analytical macro chapter, Chapter 28, meets the controversy head-on. Centered around the question of how best to model the macro economy, the chapter indicates the basic choices that new Keynesian and new classical economists make in building a simple model of the economy, and why they make them. Students learn the reasons for the controversy, namely, that the data are not entirely conclusive on either side and that each of the models has strengths and weaknesses in terms of explaining features of the macro economy. When I move on to the Keynesian cross in Chapter 29, students know that they are proceeding under the new Keynesian assumptions of sticky wages and prices, and unemployed resources. They also know that there is a very different view of the macro economy to which the text will return.

CONCLUDING EMPHASIS ON AREAS OF AGREEMENT Fortunately, the new Keynesian and new classical economists have reached a consensus on the operation of the macro economy in the long run. We can speak with some confidence, therefore, about long-run issues such as the burden of running large structural budget deficits, how to control inflation, the need for credible policies, and the effects of tax policy on saving and investment in the long run. I highlight the areas of agreement in the concluding macro chapter, Chapter 38, and elsewhere, whenever appropriate.

FLEXIBLE PRESENTATION OF THE TWO VIEWS The presentation of the two views is flexible enough so that instructors who lean toward one school or the other can emphasize the material that is compatible with their own beliefs. I suppose this will be somewhat easier for new Keynesians, simply because much of the standard material in a macro principles course still retains a very definite new Keynesian bias. But new classical economists will find the building blocks of the real business cycle spelled out in sufficient detail for their needs; I do not believe many of the existing principles texts can make that claim. In any event, I definitely do not shy away from the controversy about the operation of the macro economy in the short run.

## Additional Features of the Macro Chapters

FULL DEVELOPMENT OF AS/AD MODEL DELAYED The full development of the Aggregate Supply-Aggregate Demand (AS-AD) model in terms of prices is delayed until the final chapters. This has two advantages. It avoids the confusion of carrying both the Keynesian cross and AS-AD models along simultaneously. The new Keynesian/new classical controversy is difficult enough for students to absorb without their being burdened early on with the full development of two analytical techniques. It also allows me to present the topic of money before developing the AD curve, an essential prerequisite.

FOCUS ON THE CIRCULAR FLOW OF ECONOMIC ACTIVITY The concept of the circular flow of economic activity reappears frequently as a motivational and organizational device. Fiscal and monetary policies are presented in terms of their attempt to influence the level and composition of the circular flow.

INTERNATIONAL ASPECTS OF THE MACRO ECONOMY THROUGHOUT International aspects of the macro economy are woven into the analysis throughout, beginning with the examination of the macroeconomic policy goals and running through national income accounting, the development of the Keynesian model, automatic stabilizers, the twin budget and trade deficits, net export crowding-out, and the effects of fiscal and monetary policy. The text concludes with three chapters on international trade, international finance, and developing nations that focus on the key international issues of the day.

EMPHASIS ON THE PRACTICAL DIFFICULTIES IN THE CONDUCT OF FISCAL AND MONETARY POLICY Students are made aware of the practical considerations and difficulties in the conduct of fiscal and monetary policy.

INTUITIVE PORTFOLIO APPROACH TO MONEY AND MONETARY POLICY I have chosen an intuitive and uncluttered portfolio approach to money and its effects on the economy. The portfolio approach is extended to show how fiscal policy, and aggregate demand generally, affects interest rates.

Chapters 33–36 on money and monetary policy are really quite different from similar chapters in existing texts, although they reach the same ends. They are written in response to a teaching problem: that students have more difficulty with the topic of money than with any other major topic. The reason, I believe, is that existing texts almost unanimously present students with a rash of institutional detail, all of it foreign to them, while simultaneously confronting them with a whole new set of analytical material. The results are predictable: the average student is overwhelmed.

DELAYED PRESENTATION OF INSTITUTIONAL DETAILS I find it useful in my own teaching to begin with fundamental principles and analytics and to hold off on presenting institutional details as much as possible early on. Therefore, Chapter 33 begins with a set of preliminaries. It introduces the exchange equation as an alternative way of viewing the macro economy with an eye toward illustrating the importance of money; discusses the nature of money, including the tricky notion of the demand for money; indicates what gives money value; and presents the concept of the balance sheet or T account, with illustrations of the two transactions that are especially relevant to the study of money and finance—loans and trades of existing assets. Chapter 34 then provides the institutional details necessary to understand the operation of monetary policy in the United States.

Next, in Chapter 35, I use the old monetarist portfolio approach, along with the fiction of a money rain and how consumers and businesses would react to it, to teach, simultaneously, both the determinants of the demand for money and how increases and decreases in the money supply affect the economy. I learned the portfolio approach from reading Milton Friedman, yet one does not have to be a Friedman-style monetarist (I definitely am not) to appreciate that the portfolio approach is a wonderfully intuitive way of teaching the effects of money on national income and rates of return. The actual institutional details of U.S. monetary policy involving the Fed and the depository institutions follow quite naturally thereafter. I have had great success with this general approach, precisely because it is so intuitive and uncluttered. It also happens to better integrate the material, since the portfolio approach retains the use of balance sheets throughout. They do not disappear after the money supply multiplier has been dispensed with. In Chapter 36 I use balance sheet transactions to illustrate why an increase in aggregate demand tends to increase rates of return throughout the economy.

## PEDAGOGICAL FEATURES

The text contains a large number of pedagogical features designed to stimulate student interest, to help students learn and apply the material, to help students review material once they have studied a chapter, and to reinforce the coherence of the presentation. These features, which were carefully developed based on input from scores of economics professors, are designed and crafted to avoid cluttering the text and interrupting the flow of learning.

### Within-Chapter Pedagogy

OPENING SCENARIO Each chapter opens with a scenario that draws students into the chapter and sets the stage for the concepts and material to follow.

MARGIN COMMENTS Occasional margin comments, printed in blue, ask students to reflect on the concepts being discussed, most often by requiring them to relate those concepts directly to their own experiences. The margin comments are also used to offer insightful historical notes and comments on current issues or to elaborate on a theoretical point.

LISTS OF CONCEPTS TO LEARN AND TO RECALL Each chapter title page contains a list of Concepts to Learn that presents the learning objectives for the chapter. The Concepts to Learn list is immediately followed by a list of Concepts to Recall that alerts students to concepts from preceding chapters that they will need in order to understand the new material, and indicates where the concepts have appeared earlier.

MARGIN DEFINITIONS Definitions of key terms appear in the margins.

DETAILED FIGURE CAPTIONS Each figure contains a detailed caption that guides the student carefully through the figure and summarizes its key point.

CONCEPT SUMMARY TABLES Concept Summary tables are used where appropriate to pull together key concepts and show their overall relationship to the topic.

END-OF-CHAPTER MATERIAL End-of-chapter material includes a summary that reviews the architecture of the chapter and also provides a numbered list of key points, a list of key terms and concepts from the chapter, and questions and problems to test the student's understanding, ranging from questions calling for straight feedback to problems requiring analysis and synthesis.

The combination of margin definitions, detailed figure captions, Concept Summary tables, and the end-of-chapter material should help students to recall the main points of the chapter as they review the material.

## Additional Special Features

CASES AND ECONOMIC ADVISOR'S REPORTS A Case and Economic Advisor's Report at the end of each part places students in the role of economist, by requiring them to apply concepts and theories to realistic consulting situations. These cases ask students to make recommendations and provide advice to "clients," based on the chapter material. Each case has an international aspect to it.

LOGO SECTIONS ON INTERNATIONAL PERSPECTIVES (MICRO) AND THE SPENDING MULTIPLIER IN THE UNITED STATES (MACRO) Occasional sections in the micro chapters, approximately one for each main part, offer an international perspective on selected issues. They are identified with the logo

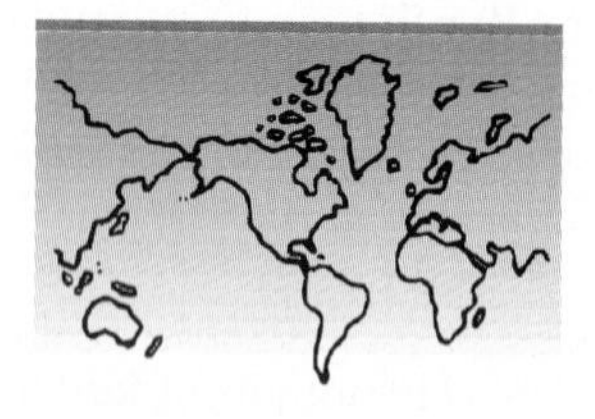

Occasional sections in the macro chapters indicate how certain features of the macro economy affect the value of the simple spending multiplier in the United States. They are identified with the logo

## Suggestions for Alternative Courses

The text is flexible enough to be used in courses organized in a number of different ways. Following are some organizational suggestions for various principles courses.

A MACRO-FIRST, YEAR-LONG COURSE Those instructors who teach macroeconomics before microeconomics should have no trouble teaching out of the text. The introductory chapters were written with an eye toward introducing both micro and macro courses. In particular, I introduce the macroeconomic policy goals in Chapter 2 and the circular flow of economic activity in Chapter 4. Chapter 4 also offers an overview of the U.S. economy that provides useful background information for a course in macroeconomics. Macro-first instructors will undoubtedly not want to cover all five chapters on supply and demand. Instead, I would recommend Chapter 5, Chapter 6 (all but the middle section), and the first half of Chapter 7 as an adequate introduction that analyzes how competitive markets operate and presents the concept of elasticity. Time permitting, some applications could be added from Chapters 8 and 9: for example, in Chapter 8, the analysis of how markets respond to taxation. Alternatively, instructors could choose the introductory chapter on the Laws of Supply and Demand in the paperback split *Principles of Macroeconomics,* which comprises the above-mentioned material from Chapters 5, 6 and 7 of the full text.

A ONE-SEMESTER COURSE, IN EITHER MICRO OR MACRO The text is available in paperback splits, *Principles of Microeconomics* and *Principles of Macroeconomics,* for one-semester courses.

A ONE-SEMESTER COURSE THAT COVERS BOTH MICRO AND MACRO The following chapters would be appropriate for a combined micro-macro course:

- Introduction: Chapters 1–4
- Micro: Chapters 5–9, 10, 11, 13, 14, 23, and 24
- Macro: Chapters 25–27, 29, 30, 33–36, 38, and 39

# SUPPLEMENTARY MATERIALS

The text is accompanied by an impressive array of supplements for instructors and for students.

## For Instructors

INSTRUCTOR'S MANUAL (Charles G. Leathers, University of Alabama-Tuscaloosa) The Instructor's Manual contains teaching objectives and a teaching outline, other organizational options, teaching hints, alternate examples including numerical examples, answers to end-of-chapter and between-part cases, additional essay and discussion questions, and teaching notes for the graphing supplement. The Instructor's Manual also includes a special note on where and how my text differs from others and a guide to using the supplement package that includes, for the graphing supplement, a set of teaching notes and, for the alternate topics, a set of objectives, teaching notes, an outline, teaching hints, supplemental readings (formatted on perforated pages), discussion questions, additional suggested readings, and transparency masters.

TEST BANK (Richard Long, Georgia State University) The Test Bank contains over 5,000 multiple choice, true/false, fill-in-the-blank, short answer, and essay questions. Questions are classified as easy, medium, or hard and are categorized as analytical or factual. A chapter-opening matrix directs instructors to specific content areas should they wish to test more heavily on particular topics. Questions are also provided for the alternate topics.

TRANSPARENCY MASTERS Transparency masters are available for all the figures in the text. Acetates for the key figures are also available.

WESTEST 3.0 Westest 3.0 is a computerized testing program for DOS, Windows, or Macintosh that allows instructors to create, edit, store, and print exams. Instructors can prepare exams by copying questions to an exam window individually, as part of a sequential range, by using a numerical select, or by generating question lists randomly. Features similar to those of word processing programs also allow instructors to add and edit questions directly on-screen. Exam questions can be arranged randomly, automatically by type (*e.g.*, true/false, multiple choice, etc.), or manually onscreen. Graphics are visible in the flow of the text.

WEST'S CLASSROOM MANAGEMENT SOFTWARE West's Classroom Management Software, included in Westest 3.0, lets instructors record and store student data and keep track of homework and project assignments and scores, exam scores, and class grades and ranking. Instructors can generate individual reports which graph a student's scores against the class average; (document missing assignments by assignment or student; provide class summaries to show grade distribution; and generate class listings of all students according to I.D. numbers, average scores, and overall grades.

ASTOUND PRESENTATION SOFTWARE Astound Presentation Software is perfect for economics classes. Astound allows instructors to manipulate graphs live during class, showing the actual movement of shifts to illustrate changes due to economic factors. Bruce McClung (Southwest Texas State University) has created electronic transparency masters for use with Astound that include the teaching outlines and all major graphics in the text.

WEST'S VIDEODISC FOR ECONOMICS West's Videodisc for Economics provides quick access to key illustrations, animated graphics, and photographs, as well as footage from the Economics U$A series by Annenberg CPB. The Videodisc format allows instructors to present graphs in a series of steps, allowing for a more gradual and easy-to-follow presentation.

WEST'S VIDEO LIBRARY FOR ECONOMICS West's Video Library for Economics includes critical thinking videos that challenge students to apply economic terms to other aspects of their world, and a series of thematic videos that deal with the deficit, the global economy, and the economics of the natural environment. An Instructor's Manual for the Video Library includes lecture notes on the videos.

## For Students

STUDY GUIDE (Lynda Rush, California State Polytechnic University-Pomona) The study guide includes learning objectives, chapter reviews, hints and cautions for the student, concepts to recall, pre- and post-tests with answers, demonstration problems, true/false, multiple choice, and short answer questions, and guides to specific problems for individual improvement in particular areas of weakness.

SPANISH GLOSSARY A Spanish Glossary is available to help Spanish-speaking students understand the key terms crucial to economics.

GRAPHING SUPPLEMENT (Colin Linsley, St. John Fisher College, and Gary E. Maggs, St. John Fisher College) The graphing supplement, which comes shrink-wrapped with the text, is an extensive supplement that shows students how to read graphs, describes how graphs are used in economic analysis, and explains the algebra behind the graphs. It also includes exercises through which students can test their knowledge of the material.

ALTERNATE TOPICS AND CASES BOOKLET The booklet covers key topics in both micro and macro.

*ALTERNATE TOPICS:*

- Khosrow Doroodian, Ohio University
  IMF Stabilization Policies in Developing Countries
- Barbara M. Fraumeni, Northweastern University/Harvard University
  Productivity and Economic Growth
- Patrick D. Mauldin, Emory University
  An Economic Perspective on Health Care Expenditures
- Joseph Pelzman, George Washington University
  Building a Market Based System: The Case of the Former Soviet Union
- David R. Schlow, Pennsylvania State University
  A Historical Perspective on Discretionary Fiscal Policy and Monetary Policy: 1930–1993
  Peter M. Schwarz, University of North Carolina-Charlotte
  The Great Depression: What Caused It and Why Did It Last So Long?
- Paul M. Taube, University of Texas-Pan American
  Defense Cuts and Their Economic Impact
- By the author
  The Bertrand Paradox and the Need to Soften Competition
  Additional Topics in Cost-Benefit Analysis
  Tax Loopholes
  Comparable Worth
  The Trade-off between Efficiency and Equity in Taxation
  Fiscal Federalism: The Economic Functions of the National, State, and Local Governments
  Forward Exchange Rates, Interest Rates, and Speculation
  The Setting of U.S. Postal Rates
  Some Pitfalls in Interpreting Data on the Distribution of Income
  The Kinked Demand Curve
  The Lucas Price Surprise Model
  Defense Contracting
  Noneconomic Factors and the Distribution of Income and Wealth
  Investment as a Strategic Variable

*ALTERNATIVE CASES (ECONOMIC ADVISOR'S REPORTS)*

- Manfred W. Keil, Northeastern University
  Unemployment in Canada
  Macroeconomic Policy and Political Interactions
  Is Inflation Bad? International Evidence
  Convergence across States to Assess the Likelihood of Convergence across Countries
- James J. McLain, University of New Orleans
  2001: A Case Odyssey—In Investment
- George Plesko, Northeastern University
  Turning Swords into Plowshares??
  How Much Should Americans Pay for Gasoline?
  Why Pay More?
  Should Gillette Be Allowed to Buy Parker?
  How Much Should Water Cost?
  Can Government Affect Savings?

ECONOMIC$ STUDY WIZARD SOFTWARE 2.0 This software package contains graphics tutorials for both micro and macro that allow students to trace the development of a graph from start to finish; terms and definitions; a review for the final exam; a special module that introduces students to leading economists and their theories and ideas; and Quizmaster, an interactive review that randomly generates multiple choice, true/false, or completion questions. Study Wizard runs on IBM PCs and compatibles. Graphics tutorials require a color monitor.

## ACKNOWLEDGMENTS

A Principles text is truly a joint product. I wish to acknowledge the contributions of the following people, and express to them my thanks and deepest gratitude.

*JONATHAN WIGHT, UNIVERSITY OF RICHMOND,* who brought closure to the text with a marvelous final chapter on The Developing Countries. Jonathan has set down the major economic problems facing these countries in clear and lively text that both students and their instructors will enjoy reading.

*THE EXCELLENT GRADUATE STUDENTS AT BOSTON COLLEGE* who helped with the preparation of the text:

- Those who assisted me with the background research: James Bathgate, Sirhan Ciftcioglu, Thomas Duggan, Elizabeth Hill, and Sr. Beth Anne Tercek.

- Those who assisted me in developing the end-of-chapter questions and the margin definitions: Basma Bekdache, Scott Browne, James Fetzer, Gurcan Gulen, Michael Kozy, Meral Karasulu, Brendan Lowney, David Richardson, Niloufer Sohrabji, and Gulcan Unal.

*MY FACULTY COLLEAGUES AT BOSTON COLLEGE,* who were a ready and willing source of expert advice on so many topics. Without meaning to slight anyone, I want to acknowledge the following for their advice and support: Kit Baum, David Belsley, Frank Gollop, Peter Gottschalk, Frank McLaughlin, Bob Murphy, and Steve Polaski.

*THE PROFESSIONALS AT WEST PUBLISHING COMPANY,* and to those associated with West, who helped with the production of the text. Many thanks to:

- Richard Fenton and Nancy Hill-Whilton, my editors, who gave me the greatest gift a Principles author can have—they let me write the book I wanted to write. They also have wonderful instincts for useful pedagogical and supplemental materials for an introductory text, and I followed their advice on these matters without exception. I look forward to working with Sharon Adams, who joined the project near the end and who will now be my editor.
- Thomas Modl, my production editor, who somehow brought all the elements of this complex project together under an extremely tight production schedule. I am moved to say that Nancy Hill-Whilton and Tom Modl worked harder on this project than I could possibly have imagined, and certainly harder than I had any right to expect.
- Sherry Goldbecker, my copy editor, whose suggestions improved the original manuscript immeasurably.
- Randy Miyake, the artist who, working from my wretched hand drawings, produced the beautiful figures for the text.
- John Tuvey, my promotion manager, who developed a thoroughly professional marketing campaign, and who kept writing such nice things about me and the text.

*THE ECONOMISTS WHO PRODUCED SUCH EXCELLENT SUPPORTING MATERIAL* for the text. The authors of the cases and Economic Advisor's Reports that appear in the text:

- Klaus G. Becker, Texas Tech University
  Will the North American Free Trade Agreement (NAFTA) Hurt the U.S. Textile Industry?
  Bringing Home the Gold and Then Some
  Some Skies Are Contestable, Others Are Not
- David Denslow, University of Florida
  The Falling Wages of High School Graduates
  Hard Times in California
  What Caused the Inflation of the 1970s?
- K. K. Fung, Memphis State University
  A Free Ride to Cross-border Shopping
  The "Flipper" Factor in International Trade
- Manfred W. Keil, Northeastern University
  An International Comparison of Unemployment Rates
- James J. McLain, University of New Orleans
  The Accord of 2006: The End of Fiscal Policy?

The first-rate supplementary materials

- Instructor's Manual, Charles G. Leathers, University of Alabama-Tuscaloosa
- Test Bank, Richard Long, Georgia State University
- Study Guide, Lynda Rush, California State Polytechnic University-Pomona
- Spanish Glossary, Carol Clark, Guilford College, and Alejandro Velez, Coordinator of Latin American Studies, St. Mary's University, San Antonio, Texas.
- Graphing Supplement, Colin Linsley, St. John Fisher College, and Gary Maggs, St. John Fisher College
- Electronic Transparency Masters, Bruce McClung, Southwest Texas State University

The Alternate Topics (I am pleased, and proud, to say that every author is a recognized expert on his or her topic):

- Khosrow Doroodian, Ohio University
- Barbara M. Fraumeni, Northeastern University/Harvard University
- Patrick D. Mauldin, Emory University
- Joseph Pelzman, George Washington University
- David R. Schlow, Pennsylvania State University
- Peter M. Schwarz, University of North Carolina at Charlotte
- Paul M. Taube, University of Texas-Pan Americ

The Alternate Cases and Economic Advisor's Re

- Manfred W. Keil, Northeastern University
- James J. McLain, University of New Orl
- George Plesko, Northeastern Universit

*THOSE WHO SERVED AS ACCURACY REVIE*[S]

- Robert Gillette, Texas A & M [U]niversity, who reviewed the figures. Robert w[as] invaluable help to me on a very difficult assig[nme]nt.

- Roy Van Til, University of Maine-Farmington, who reviewed all numerical data, calculations, and exercises. Roy also took it upon himself to read and comment on the entire manuscript. Among other things, he kept my biases firmly in check when they began to show, which helped me produce a more balanced presentation. I am deeply grateful to him.

*THE MANUSCRIPT REVIEWERS* who without exception read the chapters carefully and offered many sensible comments, criticisms, and suggestions. Although I could not incorporate all their ideas, I followed closely the thrust of their comments and the book is much better for my having done so:

Glen Atkinson, University of Nevada-Reno
Chris A. Austin, Normandale Community College
Werner Baer, University of Illinois at Urbana-Champaign
Klaus G. Becker, Texas Tech University
Roberto Bosnifaz, Babson College
Kathleen K. Bromley, Monroe Community College
Maureen Burton, California State Polytechnic University-Pomona
Carol Clark, Guilford College
Paul A. Coomes, University of Louisville
Joyce Cooper, Boston University
Joanna Cruse, Miami Dade Community College
David Denslow, University of Florida
Burton W. DeVeau, Ohio University
John Eckalbar, California State University-Chico
Robert Evans, Brandeis University
Michael J. Ferrantino, Southern Methodist University
Rodney Fort, Washington State University
Andrew W. Foshee, McNeese State University
K. K. Fung, Memphis State University
Robert Gillette, Texas A & M University
Edward C. Koziara, Drexel University
Charles G. Leathers, University of Alabama-Tuscaloosa
Stephen E. Lile, Western Kentucky University
Colin A. Linsley, St. John Fisher College
Richard Long, Georgia State University
ruce McClung, Southwest Texas State University
na L. McCoy, Truckee Meadows Community llege
cCrea, Lansing Community College
James J. McLain, University of New Orleans
Andrew Morrison, Tufts University
Kathryn A. Nantz, Fairfield University
Patrick B. O'Neill, University of North Dakota
Jan Palmer, Ohio University
George Plesko, Northeastern University
James E. Price, Syracuse University
Robert C. Puth, University of New Hampshire
Christine Rider, St. John's University
Lynda Rush, California State Polytechnic University-Pomona
P. Snoonian, University of Massachusetts-Lowell
James A. Stephenson, Iowa State University
Jack W. Thornton, East Carolina University
Gerald D. Toland, Southwest State University
Charles Tontar, Merrimack College
Alice Trost, University of Massachusetts-Boston
David A. Wells, University of Arizona
Jonathan B. Wight, University of Richmond
William D. Witter, University of North Texas.

Finally, a heartfelt thanks to all my former teachers in high school, at Williams College, and at MIT. I will mention a few names, again without meaning to slight anyone. Anthony "Dave" Davidowski, my brilliant high school math teacher, introduced me and my friends to the power and the rewards of the intellectual life. Thanks to Davidowski, I believe I knew by the age of sixteen that I would become an academic. I had many fine teachers at Williams College, but none better or more engaging than William Rhoads, then a member of the economics department. No less a scholar than Charles Kindleberger said of Rhoads: "Bill must surely be the last Renaissance man. He knows everything." Three members of the MIT economics faculty, Franco Modigliani, Peter Diamond, and Nan Friedlaender, are particularly special to me. Franco's infectious enthusiasm for economics swept me along into the discipline. Peter taught me public sector economics, my field of specialty, and what a head start he gave me. Peter delivered brilliant and original lectures, class after class, that were nowhere to be found except in the recesses of his mind. And Nan's encouragement and support as I started my career at Boston College meant more to me than she could have imagined. May God bless her.

PART

# I

# Introduction

CHAPTER

# 1

# The First Principles of Economics

## LEARNING OBJECTIVES

### CONCEPTS TO LEARN

- The three-part economic problem
- The three key players in the economy
- Interdependence
- Opportunity cost
- Economic exchange

*You are about to begin the study of economics, a subject that has achieved a commanding presence in U.S. society. When the polling organizations ask people each year what the most pressing problem facing the nation is, they most often name inflation or unemployment, both economic problems. Bill Clinton and Ross Perot kept the 1992 presidential campaign tightly focused on economic issues. They knew that elections are often won and lost on the performance of the economy and that President Bush was vulnerable on that score. Both during and after the 1992 election, President Clinton promised that economic issues would occupy center stage in his administration. The president made this promise to a nation that is bombarded daily with economic news:* THE NATIONAL DEBT EXCEEDS $4 TRILLION—UNEMPLOYMENT RISES FOR THE THIRD STRAIGHT MONTH—ANOTHER LARGE THRIFT INSTITUTION FAILS—U.S.-JAPANESE TRADE DEFICIT WORSENS—MORTGAGE RATES ON THE RISE—FED CHAIRMAN TO EASE UP ON THE MONEY SUPPLY—*Details at 11:00.*

*The general interest in economic events has swept economists into the public limelight. They are interviewed regularly on television, and they write feature columns in many of the major city newspapers. A Nobel Memorial Prize in economics has been awarded annually since 1969; no other social science has been so honored.*

What is economics that it should command so much attention?

Economics, first of all, is classified as a social science because it is concerned with the structure of society and the activities and interrelationships of individuals and groups within society. Anthropology, law, political science, psychology, and sociology are also classified as social sciences for the same reason. How is the discipline of economics distinct from these other disciplines?

Alfred Marshall, the leading economist of the early 1900s, said that economics is primarily concerned with the material requirements of personal well-being attained through the ordinary business of life. He was referring to such everyday matters as how we earn a living, what goods and services we buy, what products business firms choose to produce and how they produce them, and what services we want our governments to provide. Marshall believed that the study of these issues distinguished economics from the other social sciences, and most people today no doubt think of economics just as Marshall did. But the dividing line between economics and the other social sciences has become increasingly blurred since Marshall's day. The economic journals of the past year contain articles on welfare dependency, voting patterns in legislatures, divorce, language as a basis for discrimination, the selection of arbitrators in labor disputes, placement of a dollar value on the loss of life, and how information flows through government bureaucracies. These subjects hardly constitute what Marshall had in mind by the ordinary business of life. They seem more closely associated with what is commonly understood to be law, political science, psychology, and sociology, as the case may be. In fact, economics and the other social sciences are increasingly addressing similar issues; they are no longer so easy to distinguish on the basis of what they study.

If economics retains a distinctive identity among the social sciences, it is more by virtue of *how* it studies society and social relationships than by *what* it studies. Economists have contributed a systematic approach to the analysis of human behavior that has proved to be extremely useful and enlightening in a wide variety of applications. This approach, and the undeniable fact that most people have an abiding interest in their personal well-being and the ordinary business of life, goes far in explaining the current interest in economics.

For the beginning student, then, the key to understanding economics lies in understanding its fundamental principles of analysis. These principles are so important that the first four chapters will serve as an introduction to them. They need not be mastered at this point, but it is essential to meet the fundamental principles before attempting to analyze and interpret the important economic events and issues of the day. They appear time and again throughout the text and serve as the threads that tie economics together. Perhaps the best gauge of your progress in the course is whether you believe you are becoming more familiar with these principles as you proceed through the text from topic to topic.

## THE ECONOMIC PROBLEM

The first principle of economic analysis is that every economic problem has an identical three-part structure consisting of *objectives*, *alternatives*, and *constraints*. Each part of the economic problem is equally necessary. Take away any one of them and the economic problem disappears.

THE ECONOMIC PROBLEM
A three-part problem consisting of objectives, alternatives, and constraints.

*Objectives:* People must have **objectives,** or goals, to have an economic problem; they must care about the consequences of their decisions. Of course, we do have objectives in all aspects of our lives. We care about what goods and services we buy, how we earn our living, what kind of education we receive, how we spend our free time, and so forth. We want to do as well as we can in whatever we do.

OBJECTIVES
The part of the economic problem that refers to the goals that economic agents try to achieve.

Zonker Harris in the "Doonesbury" comic strip offers a striking contrast to the rest of us. Zonker appears to go through life without a care in the world, which makes him one of the happiest characters on the comic strip pages. More power to him. He is happy in large part because his carefree attitude frees him from ever having an economic problem. We are not so fortunate.

*Alternatives:* The term **alternatives** refers to the necessity of making choices. We must have more than one way of reaching our objectives. There can be no problem without choice because then there is no decision to be made. We would simply do the best we can by following the single available option.

ALTERNATIVES
The part of the economic problem that refers to the necessity of making choices.

Traditional peasant societies are tightly ruled by customs handed down through the ages. The people behave as they do largely because that is how their ancestors behaved. They face a limited range of economic problems as a result. In modern industrialized societies each generation is far more likely to set out on its own because economic development gives people the freedom to make new choices. Increased choice does not necessarily bring increased happiness, however, as any number of social scientists have noted. One consequence of our freedom to choose is that we are forced to confront the economic problem more frequently.

*Constraints:* **Constraints** that people face in trying to achieve their objectives form the final pillar in the structure of all economic problems. The idea of being constrained has a very precise meaning in economic analysis: No matter how cleverly we choose among the alternatives open to us, we cannot fully achieve our objectives. We always come up a little short when trying to solve our economic problems, which explains why confronting the economic problem is not usually a happy experience.

CONSTRAINTS
The part of the economic problem that refers to the limitations that prevent economic agents from achieving their objectives.

We often do achieve particular objectives, of course. You will soon earn that college degree. Some people who want the good life do eventually buy that mansion high on the hill. Whenever we achieve a particular objective, we no longer have an economic problem relating to it because we are no longer constrained in pursuing it. No one fully escapes the economic problem, however. We always want more out of life than we are able to achieve.

The most common way of describing the notion of constraints is to say that we have limited, or scarce, resources. The **Law of Scarcity** is a fundamental principle of economics. It says that resources are scarce in the sense that they are not sufficient to achieve the stated objectives, or goals. For instance, suppose that you aspire to all the trappings of the good life: fine cars, a beautiful home, stylish clothes, Caribbean vacations, and the like. The Law of Scarcity applies to you so long as you cannot afford all the things you want. In other words, you continue to have an economic problem.

LAW OF SCARCITY

The principle that resources are not sufficient to achieve all the objectives, or goals, of an economic problem.

REFLECTION: Test your understanding of the economic problem by thinking about the economic problem of your college or university. What are some of its objectives, alternatives, and constraints?

The three-part economic problem—objectives, alternatives, constraints—is so central to economics that it provides the most widely accepted short definition of economics itself. Economics is the study of how best to allocate scarce resources. In the definition, "allocate" refers to choosing among the alternatives, "scarce resources" refers to the constraints, and "best" implicitly captures the idea that people are trying to achieve various objectives, or goals.

## THE KEY PLAYERS IN THE ECONOMY

The key players in an economy are the individual, the business firm, and the government. We will begin with the individual and the business firm because they define the roles that economic actors or agents can have in any economy. Government agencies play both parts, sometimes acting as individuals do and sometimes acting as business firms do.

Individuals perform two basic economic functions. On the one hand, they purchase most of the final goods and services produced by business firms. ("Final" goods and services are those that require no further processing, such as bread, shirts, and automobiles.) Economists refer to individuals in this role as **consumers** because people consume goods and services as they use them. On the other hand, individuals supply resources that they own to the business firms, which the firms then use to produce goods and services. Economists refer to these resources as **factors of production** because they serve as inputs into the production process. Individuals supply the three *primary* factors of production: labor, land, and capital.

CONSUMERS

Economic agents who consume goods and services and who supply the primary factors of production—labor, capital, and land—to producers.

FACTORS OF PRODUCTION

The resources or inputs that producers use to produce goods and services, consisting of labor, capital, land, and material inputs.

**Labor** is a catch-all term referring to all the different kinds of skills and occupations found in the work force—blue-collar employees such as manual laborers; white-collar employees such as clerks, secretaries, and managers; professionals such as lawyers, doctors, and teachers; and **entrepreneurs,** those imaginative individuals who bring new ideas to the business world and are willing to take the risk of starting new ventures or businesses.

LABOR

A catch-all term referring to all the different kinds of skills and occupations found in the work force; one of the primary factors of production.

ENTREPRENEURS

Imaginative individuals who bring new ideas to the business world and who are willing to take the risks of starting new ventures or businesses.

Individuals own and supply the **land** on which business firms build their factories and offices. *Land* also refers to the contents of the land, the fertile soil and the natural resources—minerals, natural gas, and oil—which are themselves important factors of production.

**Capital** refers primarily to plant and equipment, that is, the factories, buildings, and machinery that all firms require for the production of goods and services. Capital inputs have to be produced themselves, and business firms buy them directly from other business firms. But individuals supply the funds, through their savings, that enable business firms to purchase the plant and equipment.

Business firms occupy the other side of these transactions. Economists often refer to business firms as **producers** because their role is to produce the final goods and services that individuals consume. In order to do this business firms must receive factors of production from individuals and other business firms, and then decide how best to turn these inputs into goods and services. The only transactions firms engage in that do not directly involve individuals are the purchases by firms of semi-finished products, called **material inputs,** from other firms. Examples of material inputs include the grain used to make bread, the cloth used to make shirts, and the glass used in a car's windows. These material inputs are the most important factor of production for most firms. They are combined with the three primary factors of production supplied by individuals and brought to ever-higher stages of "finish." The last stage in the production hierarchy is the final good or service—the bread, shirt, and automobile.

Governments are both consumers and producers of goods and services. When the Department of Defense buys intercontinental ballistic missiles, it is engaging in an act of public consumption on behalf of all citizens. The missiles are final goods whose sole purpose is to deter foreign countries from acts of aggression against the United States. We may or may not like these missiles, but we are all forced to consume the service they provide. Governments are more often producers of goods and services. Public education, mass transportation systems, public utilities, the postal service, and the nation's highway system are all examples of goods and services that are produced and maintained by government agencies for the benefit of private individuals or business firms. Governments become involved in consuming and producing goods and services in a market economy because the market cannot always be relied on to provide the goods and services that people want. For example, individual citizens cannot easily provide for the security of an entire nation. The national government is in a much better position to formulate and carry out national security policy. Similarly, a complete network of highways is essential to any nation, yet private business firms could not profitably construct and maintain most of the highway network.

The government performs one other important function in an economy. It redistributes resources among individuals, most often to protect people from becoming impoverished or to help the less fortunate who have become impoverished. The leading example in the United States is the Social Security System, a $300 billion federal program that taxes workers through a payroll tax and transfers the proceeds to retired workers and their families in the form of monthly cash payments and hospital benefits. The result is a massive redistribution of income from the younger generations to the elderly, undertaken so that the elderly do not become wards of the state.[1]

LAND

The property on which business firms build their factories and office buildings; includes the fertile soil and natural resources contained within the land; one of the primary factors of production.

CAPITAL

The plant and equipment required to produce goods and services; one of the primary factors of production.

PRODUCERS

Economic agents who produce goods and services by receiving factors of production from consumers and other producers.

MATERIAL INPUTS

Semi-finished products purchased by firms and used as a factor of production.

## The Economic Problems of the Key Players

Before leaving the key players, let's take a brief look at some of the economic problems that they face. Understanding the economic problems of individuals, business firms, and government agencies is one of the primary goals of economic analysis.

---

[1]The Social Security System also provides monthly cash payments and hospital benefits to disabled workers and their families. The disabled are a much smaller population than are the retired elderly.

THE INDIVIDUAL We have all experienced the individual's role as a consumer of goods and services. What is the nature of our economic problem in that role, which economists refer to as the consumer's economic problem? To begin thinking about the consumer's economic problem, suppose that all decisions relating to the earning of income have been made, so that the individual has a fixed amount of income to spend. What are the consumer's objectives, alternatives, and constraints, given a fixed income?

*Objectives:* We consume goods and services for a variety of reasons, some noble, some less so. A number of motives—survival, comfort, pleasure, learning, status, and greed—come easily to mind. Economists lump all of these motives under the single term **utility,** or satisfaction. Our goal as consumers is to achieve the highest possible utility, or satisfaction, from the goods and services we purchase.

UTILITY
The value that a consumer derives from the consumption of goods and services.

*Alternatives:* Consumers make thousands of economic decisions every year of their lives. We have a bewildering variety of goods and services to choose from, and different people certainly choose very different ways of achieving satisfaction. The choices we make depend in part on our tastes or preferences, which determine how much satisfaction we receive from the goods and services we consume. Some people like fast cars, nice clothes, and dining in fine restaurants. Other people have little interest in fast cars or nice clothes and prefer to eat at home.

*Constraints:* The constraints, or scarce resources, that limit the amount of utility we can attain have two distinct components. On the one hand, everyone has limited income from which to purchase goods and services (wealth, the accumulation of all past saving, can be included along with income). On the other hand, all goods and services come with prices that reflect the costs of producing them. The combination of limited income and prices means that our purchases of goods and services must ultimately come to an end. Moreover, when consumers have made all their purchases they are not entirely satisfied, with rare exceptions. They would like to have bought even more. This is the test that consumers are effectively constrained, subject to the Law of Scarcity; they have not escaped the economic problem.

We have ignored all decisions related to the earning of income to this point. Once these are brought into the picture, the consumer's economic problem changes in both structure and complexity.

Consider the decision to work. To keep matters simple, suppose the individual will only work at one type of job and is deciding how much time to spend working at that job. The job pays an hourly wage. Notice how the economic problem changes form. Income is no longer a part of the constraint. Rather, deciding how much income to earn becomes one of the alternatives. Time is now the limited resource—there are only so many hours in the day to be spent working or not working. Also, the wage rate offered on the job becomes an important price. It is essentially the price or cost of time because it determines the dollars of income sacrificed for each hour the individual chooses not to work.

REFLECTION: Students understand as well as anyone that time is a scarce resource. Do you feel constrained more often by limited income or limited time?

A final complication in the consumer's economic problem arises whenever individuals decide to save some income, instead of consuming all of it. The decision to save introduces a time element into the consumer's decision process because saving is essentially a decision to forego current consumption for consumption sometime in the future. Saving changes both the objective and the alternatives as consumers think about purchasing goods and services over a number of years, not just one year. Saving also changes the consumer's constraint by providing additional income from the returns to the saving. It introduces a whole new set of prices in the form of interest rates and other rates of return that determine how much future consumption can be obtained for each dollar of current consumption sacrificed by saving.

THE BUSINESS FIRM Although we are all consumers, most of us have not had experience managing a business firm. Nonetheless, even the most casual knowledge of business is enough to appreciate that "doing business" involves solving the economic problem.

*Objectives:* The objective that comes immediately to mind when thinking about the business firm operating in a market economy is **profit,** the difference between the revenue obtained from selling goods and services and the cost of producing them. In fact, much economic analysis of business behavior assumes that making a profit is the only objective of the firm. This is surely an overstatement, however. Managers of firms are also concerned with market share, sales growth, and even good will within the community. Nonetheless, profit is certainly the predominant goal of U.S. business.

PROFIT
The difference between the revenue obtained from selling goods and services and the cost of producing them.

*Alternatives:* Business firms face three distinct choices. They must decide *what* goods and services to produce, and then *how many* of each to produce. They must also decide *how* to produce their products. Most products can be produced in many different ways, and similar products are often produced quite differently in different parts of the world, and even within the same country. Some firms choose highly skilled labor operating the newest, most sophisticated machinery. Other firms choose older equipment and employ less skilled labor to operate it.

*Constraints:* Finally, all business firms encounter constraints in their pursuit of profit. On the revenue side, consumers will buy only so much of any one firm's product, no matter what the price. Consumers' budgets are limited, and they can often buy a similar product from another firm. Therefore, the total revenue from sales is naturally limited. On the cost side, a given amount of inputs can only produce so much output, no matter how efficient the firm is. Also, all inputs come with prices, so that input costs rise as firms expand their production. Therefore, attempts to increase profit by expanding production are squeezed on both the revenue and the cost sides: Revenues are limited, but costs continue to rise. The result of the revenue-cost squeeze is that business firms cannot escape the economic problem either. After the managers have made all their decisions as best they can, they still wish they had earned a larger profit.

GOVERNMENT AGENCIES All government agencies, from the smallest town department to the giant Department of Defense, must confront the economic problem. Consider briefly the objectives, alternatives, and constraints of the Department of Defense.

*Objectives:* The broad goal of achieving national security has a number of specific components. The United States wants to deter acts of aggression against it. It also wants the flexibility to respond to aggression in the Middle East, Western Europe, and the Western Hemisphere, at the very least.

*Alternatives:* The Defense Department has a number of options in pursuing each of its objectives. For starters, it must decide what role each branch of the armed services should play in the different parts of the world and how best to equip the armed services for their missions.

*Constraints:* Even the mighty Defense Department is given a fixed budget by the administration and Congress. It is certainly constrained in trying to meet its numerous objectives. The ultimate constraint on all government agencies is the need to raise taxes to finance government activity. Citizens are willing to pay taxes, but only to a certain extent.

### Other Examples of the Economic Problem

The economic problem appears in all walks of life, which explains why economic analysis extends beyond the ordinary business of life into areas traditionally associated with the other social sciences. Think about a politician trying to gain election. The objective is victory in the election. The alternatives are the essence of campaign strategy. How much time should the candidate spend on the campaign trail and in which parts of the state or country? How much of the budget should be allocated to media advertisements, how much to mailers and other campaign literature, how much to dinners, parties, and other social engagements? What portions of the advertising budget should go to television, to radio, and to the newspapers and magazines? The constraints are limited time, limited campaign funds, and the costs of the various options.

Students also feel the pressures of the economic problem, most obviously at exam time. It is Thursday, and you have five final exams next week—two on Monday, two on Tuesday, and the last one on Wednesday. You figure that you will have 30 hours available to study for the five tests. A common objective is to maximize your grade point average by scoring as well as you can on the five tests combined. The alternatives include the choices you must make regarding how to study for each subject, how much time to allocate to the study of each subject, and in what order to study the subjects. The constraints are time and your limited knowledge of the five subjects. Few students are able to score 100 on every exam; the Law of Scarcity applies to nearly every student.

A moment's reflection should be enough to appreciate how pervasive the economic problem is. A key point to derive from our examples is that an economic analysis of any problem begins by defining the structure of the problem in terms of three main components: What are the objectives? The alternatives? The constraints? What is the relationship between the alternatives and both the objectives and the constraints? How will a particular choice help in meeting the objectives? To what extent will it use up scarce resources? Once a problem is described in this fashion, the same set of economic principles can be applied to solving it. The actual issue or context does not really matter because all problems that can be structured as the economic problem are analytically equivalent. This is why we will begin each new topic area in this text with a discussion of its structure in terms of objectives, alternatives, and constraints. Understanding an issue as an economic problem is the first step toward understanding how to analyze it.

## TWO PRINCIPLES STEMMING FROM THE ECONOMIC PROBLEM

Two important principles apply to all economic problems: interdependence and the meaning of cost as opportunity cost. Each follows directly from the structure of the economic problem.

## Interdependence

The principle of **interdependence** says that economic decisions are interrelated. The consequences of a decision always spread beyond the immediate objectives of the decision. The structure of the economic problem guarantees this principle simply because any decision uses scarce resources. Whenever scarce resources have been expended, a decision to do something necessarily implies a decision not to do something else. As a result, any one decision always has at least two consequences: the benefit, in terms of the objectives, of the decision to do something; and the loss, also in terms of the objectives, of the decision not to do something else.

INTERDEPENDENCE
The principle that economic decisions are interrelated such that the consequences of a decision always spread beyond the immediate objectives of the decision.

The principle of interdependence will be clear if the structure of the economic problem is kept firmly in mind. For example, voters have learned to discount the promises of politicians seeking election. "If I am elected, we will have better schools, smoother highways, expanded recreational facilities, and no new taxes." People know that something has to give because they recognize the principle of interdependence. If we do get better public services, then we will almost certainly pay higher taxes. Or we might get better schools and no new taxes, but then watch out for the potholes. Regarding your own economic problem as a consumer, you know when you are buying those new winter clothes that you will probably have to cut back on entertainment for awhile. When you are studying for final exams, the principle of interdependence is also evident, sometimes painfully so. You may choose to study hard for the biology final and pray that the history final will be easy.

## Opportunity Cost

What does something cost? The answer to this question depends on the context in which it is being asked. Cost is usually defined as an absolute concept in everyday conversation, the purchase price of an item. For example, suppose that you are wearing a watch and someone asks you how much the watch cost. Your natural response would be to state the price of the watch, say, $75.00.

Sometimes, though, we add a relative sense to the notion of cost. If you happen to be a millionaire, you might respond: "Not much, only $75." If you happen to have only a small annual income, you might respond: "The watch was very expensive. It cost me $75." The words "not much" and "very expensive" are defining the cost of the watch in a relative sense. You are implicitly comparing the price of the watch relative to the resources that you have.

The relative meaning of cost is the one used in economic analysis. Economists always compare the prices of goods and services with the resources that are available to pay for them. The relative nature of cost in economic analysis follows directly from the structure of the economic problem and the associated principle of interdependence.

According to the principle of interdependence, the decision to purchase the watch ultimately prevents you from purchasing something else. For example, suppose you were choosing between the watch and a $75 sweater, knowing that you could afford only the watch or the sweater, but not both. Therefore, the decision to buy the watch is simultaneously a decision not to buy the sweater. Under these circumstances the true *cost* of the watch can only be accounted relative to the value to you of the sweater. The value of the sweater is said to be the opportunity cost of the watch, since the sweater is the alternative or opportunity foregone by choosing the watch.

OPPORTUNITY COST
The economic meaning of cost; the value, in terms of the objectives, of the next best alternative.

In general, economists define the true economic cost, the **opportunity cost,** of any decision A as the value, in terms of the objectives, of the next best alternative B. Notice that B must be the *next best* alternative among all the possible choices because only the next best alternative determines the value of what is being sacrificed by decision A. In other words, the answer to the question "Is A worth its cost?" is yes only if the value of A in terms of the objectives exceeds the value of the next best alternative B.

The following examples illustrate the notion of opportunity cost and how it differs from common everyday notions of cost. Each example assumes that the objective is to have as much income as possible.

EXAMPLES ILLUSTRATING OPPORTUNITY COST Suppose that your rich uncle dies and leaves you the open-air parking lot he owned and operated in downtown San Francisco. After operating the parking lot yourself for a year, you discover just how nice a gift it was. It brought in $500,000 in parking revenue, with an out-of-pocket cost of only $50,000 for operators' salaries and routine maintenance and repairs. The parking lot appears to have brought you a profit of $450,000.

Is $450,000 the true profit, however? The answer from an economic point of view is certainly no because there is a large, hidden opportunity cost of using the land as a parking lot. Land in downtown San Francisco is extremely valuable as a site for office or apartment buildings. Suppose that a developer were willing to offer you $10 million for the land. Selling the land and placing the $10 million in a bank account that offers a 5 percent rate of interest would bring an annual income of $500,000, $50,000 more than the profit from operating a parking lot on the land.

By an economic accounting, then, the parking lot actually loses $50,000 per year: The value of the land as a parking lot is $50,000 less than the value in its next best alternative. Your tax accountant, however, will have to record a profit on the parking lot of $450,000, or you may wind up in jail. Cost for tax purposes in this example is the $50,000 you spent to operate and maintain the lot. The point is that the appropriate definition of cost depends on the circumstances in which it is being used. An economist includes the $500,000 opportunity cost because the relevant economic question is "What is the best use of the land among various alternatives?" In this example using the land for an office or apartment building is more valuable than using the land as a parking lot. The tax authorities, however, do not allow you to add the $500,000 of opportunity cost to the $50,000 you spent to operate and maintain the parking lot.

Your college education is another good example illustrating the concept of opportunity cost. Suppose that you think of your education strictly as an investment, as a means to better jobs and higher earnings for the years after college. What should be included in the annual cost of your education? The principal *out-of-pocket costs* are tuition, fees, books, room and board, supplies, other incidental living expenses, and, in some schools, a personal computer. But these are not the true economic costs, the opportunity costs.

The out-of-pocket costs and the opportunity costs of your education differ in two ways. First, the list of out-of-pocket costs misses a large opportunity cost, the wages that you could have earned had you not attended college. For students who do not work, a minimum value of those opportunity costs each year would be the minimum wage, $4.25 per hour, times 40 hours per week for 50 weeks, giving an annual sum of $8,500. And this amount understates what most young adults could actually earn today if not in college. It probably more closely represents the opportunity cost of students who are working part-time while attending college, instead of working full-time if they had not attended college.

Second, some of the out-of-pocket costs of an education, particularly room and board and incidental living expenses, would have been incurred anyway, even without attending college. True, a resident student might have lived at home for awhile if he or she had not attended college, but someone is still bearing the costs of the room and board. Since these out-of-pocket costs occur whether you attend college or not, they should be excluded from the true economic costs of obtaining the education.

Understanding the notion of cost as opportunity cost is central to proper economic analysis. It takes some practice because, as these examples illustrate, common notions of cost often differ from the economic meaning of cost. In particular, opportunity costs (for example, the $500,000 annual income from selling the parking lot to developers and the wages forgone by attending college) may differ from out-of-pocket costs, and some out-of-pocket costs (for example, payment of room and board by resident students) may not be opportunity costs.

There is only one sure way to make an accurate accounting of true economic cost. Describe as accurately as possible all elements of the economic problem under consideration, especially all relevant choices or alternatives for meeting the objectives. Economists always ask "What are the alternatives?" because the alternatives to any course of action determine the cost of that action. The playwright George Bernard Shaw understood this point regarding the difficulties of old age. When asked on his 80th birthday how it felt to be 80, he replied, "Not bad, considering the alternative."

## EXCHANGE

Individuals, business firms, and government agencies do not solve their economic problems in isolation. They engage in **exchanges** of goods, services, and factors of production with one another in all possible combinations: individuals with businesses, businesses with businesses, government agencies with businesses, and so forth. The study of these exchanges is the second main theme in economic analysis, every bit as central to economic analysis as the study of the economic problem itself. A second expanded short definition of economics combines the two main themes of the discipline. **Economics** is often defined as the study of the allocation of scarce resources through the process of exchange.

EXCHANGE
The trading of goods, services, and factors of production among the key players in the economy.

ECONOMICS
The study of the allocation of scarce resources through the process of exchange.

The number of economic exchanges is truly staggering in a large, modern economy such as that of the United States, with its more than 250 million people, 18 million business firms, and 89,000 government agencies. The total value of economic exchange in the United States each year is measured in trillions of dollars.

Economists are interested in the incentives that motivate exchanges of goods and services and factors of production. How do individuals use these exchanges to increase their utility, firms to increase their profit, and government agencies to meet their objectives? No one has to tell individuals, business firms, and government agencies to engage in exchange. They are naturally drawn into

REFLECTION: What kinds of economic exchanges have you made in the past week in your role as a consumer? In your role as a supplier of primary factors of production?

economic exchanges with one another for all manner of items. Indeed, the urge to exchange is so strong that some people are quite willing to risk the consequences of engaging in illegal exchanges. The commonplace occurrence of economic exchanges can happen only because both parties typically gain from an exchange. We want to understand how the purchase and sale of goods and services can simultaneously benefit both consumers and producers by helping each of them solve their economic problems.

Economists are also interested in the results of economic exchanges, particularly whether they promote the interests of society as a whole. The results of exchanges very much depend on the conditions under which they take place. Some exchanges involve large numbers of participants, such as the sale of milk to millions of consumers by thousands of grocery stores. Other exchanges involve only a few participants, such as the bargaining between union representatives and business managers over the union wage. Governments often intervene in exchanges between individuals and firms. Very few goods, services, and factors of production escape taxation by some government in the United States, and governments try to influence the prices at which exchanges occur through such devices as minimum wage laws, rent controls, and quotas on goods imported from other countries. We want to understand how the number of participants and the nature of government intervention can affect the benefits of economic exchanges from society's point of view.

The economic problem and the process of exchange are the two main themes in economic analysis. We will return to the principles and issues of economic exchanges in Chapter 4. Chapters 2 and 3 continue to focus on the economic problem.

## SUMMARY

Chapter 1 has provided an introduction to the two main themes of economic analysis: the economic problem and the process of exchange.

1. The economic problem has a three-part structure consisting of objectives, alternatives, and constraints.
2. The Law of Scarcity says that people are constrained in trying to solve their economic problems. They never have enough resources to meet all their objectives.
3. A widely accepted short definition of economics follows directly from the structure of the economic problem. Economics is the study of how best to allocate scarce resources.
4. The three key players in an economy are individuals, business firms, and government agencies. Individuals have the dual role of consuming goods and services and of providing factors of production to business firms. Business firms have the dual role of buying factors of production from individuals and other business firms and of producing goods and services for sale. Government agencies act as both consumers and producers in a market economy. They purchase some goods and services such as missiles on behalf of the citizens, and they produce a variety of goods and services such as public utilities and mass transit systems. Government agencies also redistribute income among individuals and business firms. All three players must confront the economic problem.

5. The principle of interdependence says that the consequences of economic decisions spread beyond the immediate concern of the decisions. The principle follows directly from the structure of the economic problem, which implies that a decision to choose one alternative is simultaneously a decision not to choose another alternative.
6. Because economic decisions are interdependent, the true economic cost of any decision is defined as an opportunity cost. The cost of any decision A is the value in terms of the objectives of the next best alternative B.
7. Individuals, business firms, and government agencies solve their economic problems by engaging in exchanges with one another.
8. A common expanded short definition of economics incorporates the two main themes of economic analysis: the economic problem and the process of exchange. Economics is the study of the allocation of scarce resources through the process of exchange.

## KEY TERMS

consumers
the economic problem
economics
exchange
factors of production
interdependence
Law of Scarcity
opportunity cost
producers
profit
utility

## QUESTIONS

1. You tell your friends that you are studying economics, and they ask, "What's economics about?" How would you answer them?
2. Give three examples of how the Law of Scarcity will affect you while taking your Principles of Economics class.
3. a. How are the principles of interdependence and opportunity cost related?
   b. Why does each principle follow directly from the three-part economic problem?
4. Name a well-known entrepreneur in the United States today, and indicate why that person is considered an entrepreneur.
5. Explain how consumers and producers are both "buyers" and "sellers" in the marketplace.
6. Suppose that you buy a ticket to a concert a month ahead of time for $20. Then you find out a week before the concert that your friends are having a big party at the same time. How will you decide whether to go to the concert or to the party? In particular, what is the opportunity cost of going to the party? Of going to the concert?
7. Look through your newspaper, and find one article that is discussing the government in its role as a producer and another article that is discussing the government in its role as a redistributor of income. Can you identify some or all of the three components of the government's economic problem in each article?
8. Describe the economic problem of buying a car in terms of its objectives, alternatives, and constraints.

CHAPTER

# 2

# Solving the Economic Problem

## LEARNING OBJECTIVES

### CONCEPTS TO LEARN

Efficiency

Process equity: equality of opportunity

End-results equity: horizontal equity

An economic model

The margin in economic analysis

Positive and normative economics

Microeconomics and macroeconomics

### CONCEPTS TO RECALL

The three-part economic problem [1]

Opportunity cost [1]

Interdependence [1]

*All students are keenly aware of the economic problem during final exams, when the problem of how to study effectively hits with full force. You may have four or five exams in one week and little time left to study for them. Some of your subjects come easily to you; others are quite difficult. The atmosphere during finals is also highly charged and stressful. Everyone is anxious, no one gets much sleep, and outside distractions such as telephone calls or stereos blaring are especially annoying. How should you go about studying for your exams with all these factors playing on your mind? What is the best solution to your studying problem?*

Chapter 2 discusses the concepts and methods that economists use to analyze and solve the economic problem wherever it appears. We will often use the economic problem of studying for exams to illustrate the material in the chapter simply because you are so familiar with it.

## SOLVING THE ECONOMIC PROBLEM: EFFICIENCY AND EQUITY

Economic analysis rests on a fundamental assumption about human nature: that people are always striving to find the best possible solutions to their own economic problems. In other words, economists assume that people are self-interested, that they try to squeeze every last personal advantage from any given situation. Although this may not seem like a terribly uplifting assumption about the human condition, it is really the only assumption that can support a unified theory of economic behavior. Economists are trying to understand and predict patterns of human behavior that apply generally to a broad range of situations. The only hope of finding such patterns rests on the assumption that people seek the best possible solutions to their economic problems. Suppose, instead, that people do not care enough about their objectives to try their best to achieve them. What, then, does motivate their behavior? No obvious answer comes to mind, and economists cannot build a consistent theory of economic behavior without knowing what motivates that behavior. In truth, people are primarily self-interested in much of what they do, which goes a long way toward explaining why economists have been fairly successful in describing their behavior.

What properties characterize the best possible solution to the economic problem? Economists judge solutions by means of two criteria, efficiency and equity, or fairness. Of the two, efficiency is the more widely applicable because it applies to all economic problems. Equity, or fairness, enters in only when the objectives of the economic problem involve the well-being of two or more people. For example, business firms want to be efficient in producing their products, and students want to be efficient in studying for their exams. Neither business firms nor students have reason to be concerned about equity in these matters. By contrast, parents may want to be both efficient and equitable (fair) in providing for their children, and a society may want to be both efficient and equitable in providing for its citizens.

Let's look closely at the criteria of efficiency and equity. They are central to the study of economics.

## Efficiency

In the broadest sense, *efficiency* means that people have made the choices that best meet their objectives. This is why the efficiency criterion applies to all economic problems and would appear to be what solving the economic problem is all about. The notion of "best meeting objectives" is deceptive, however, It is an unambiguous criterion only if the economic problem has a single objective. To see this, think about the economic problem of studying for tests.

EFFICIENCY WITH A SINGLE OBJECTIVE Suppose that you have a history test tomorrow. Your *objective* is to get 100 on the test. The *alternatives* are the various ways of studying for the test: Go over class notes, read the textbook a number of times, discuss the main issues and concepts with your friends, and so forth. The *constraints* are two-fold: You have a limited amount of time to study for the test and a limited knowledge of the subject matter. If this is truly an economic problem, then the constraints must prevent you from reaching your objective. The Law of Scarcity applies: No matter how well you study for the test, you cannot get 100. Instead, your (single) objective is to get as close to 100 as possible.

Figure 2.1 illustrates inefficient and efficient solutions to your economic problem. The possible test scores are listed on the vertical axis, with 100 the maximum possible score. The two bar graphs show the test scores you can achieve with each of two study strategies, labeled 1 and 2. Strategy 1 might involve spending most of your time discussing the issues and concepts with your friends, and strategy 2 might involve spending most of your time memorizing class notes. According to the figure, strategy 1 earns you 75 on the test, and strategy 2 earns you 85. Notice that neither strategy allows you to score 100 on the test; scoring 100 is impossible, given the nature of your economic problem.

Figure 2.1 indicates that strategy 1 is inefficient because it does not best satisfy your objective. Strategy 2 does better. (Perhaps your study group wandered too often from the course material.) Strategy 2 may or may not be efficient; we cannot tell from the information given in the figure. However, sup-

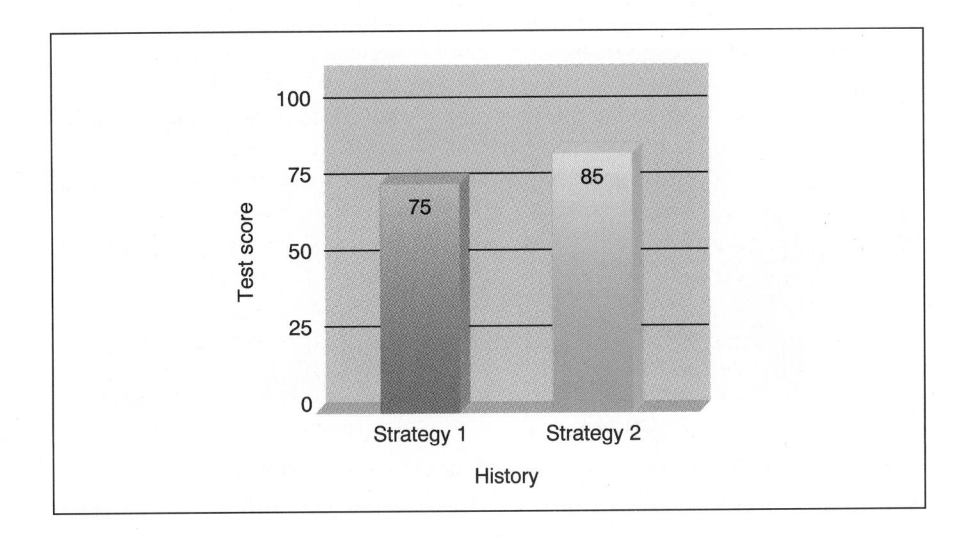


FIGURE 2.1

**Studying for a History Test**

The bar graphs show the scores achieved on a history test with two different studying strategies. Strategy 1 is inefficient; it does achieve the objective of getting as close to a 100 as possible. Strategy 2 may or may not be efficient. It is efficient if no other studying strategy can achieve a test score above an 85.

pose that you could somehow determine that no other study strategy would earn you as high a score as 85 on the test. If so, then strategy 2 is efficient—it best satisfies the single objective of scoring as close to 100 as possible.

The only wrinkle in defining efficiency when the economic problem has a single objective occurs when the objective does not have a natural limit. Consumers seek utility or satisfaction from their purchases of goods and services without any limit to the amount of utility they desire. Similarly, business firms strive to earn profits without any limit to the amount of profits they desire. In these cases, best meeting the objective means maximizing utility or profit, achieving the largest possible amount of utility or profit. The notion of maximizing the objective as the test of efficiency when the economic problem has a single objective is perfectly general. It also applies to cases in which the objective has a natural limit. In the study example, strategy 2 is efficient if 85 is the maximum possible test score that you are able to achieve.

EFFICIENCY WITH MULTIPLE OBJECTIVES The notion that a set of choices best meets objectives becomes ambiguous, however, when the economic problem has two or more objectives. To see why, suppose that you have two tests tomorrow, one in history and one in calculus. You want to do well in both subjects, so now you have two objectives, to get 100 on each test. The choices that apply to studying history apply to calculus as well, as do the constraints of limited time and knowledge. However, the second test adds a new choice to the set of alternatives, how much time to spend studying for each test. Also, the constraints of limited time and knowledge are binding: You cannot get 100 on both exams no matter how well you study. In this example, though, we will assume that you can get 100 on one of the tests if you spend enough time studying the subject and study effectively.

Figure 2.2 illustrates the ambiguity of best meeting two (or more) objectives. Each graph illustrates a possible study strategy for meeting your objectives. Now there are two objectives, getting 100 on each test.

In the first strategy you have decided to concentrate on history and let calculus slide. You study long enough to get 100 on the history test, but then you only have enough time left for calculus to get 70 on the calculus test. Remem-

FIGURE 2.2

**Studying for a History Test and a Calculus Test**

The bar graphs show the scores achieved on a hisotry test and a calculus test with three different studying strategies. No strategy allows you to score 100 on both tests. Each of the studying strategies is efficient if the Law of Substitution holds: In order to achieve a higher score on one of the tests your score on the other test must decrease.

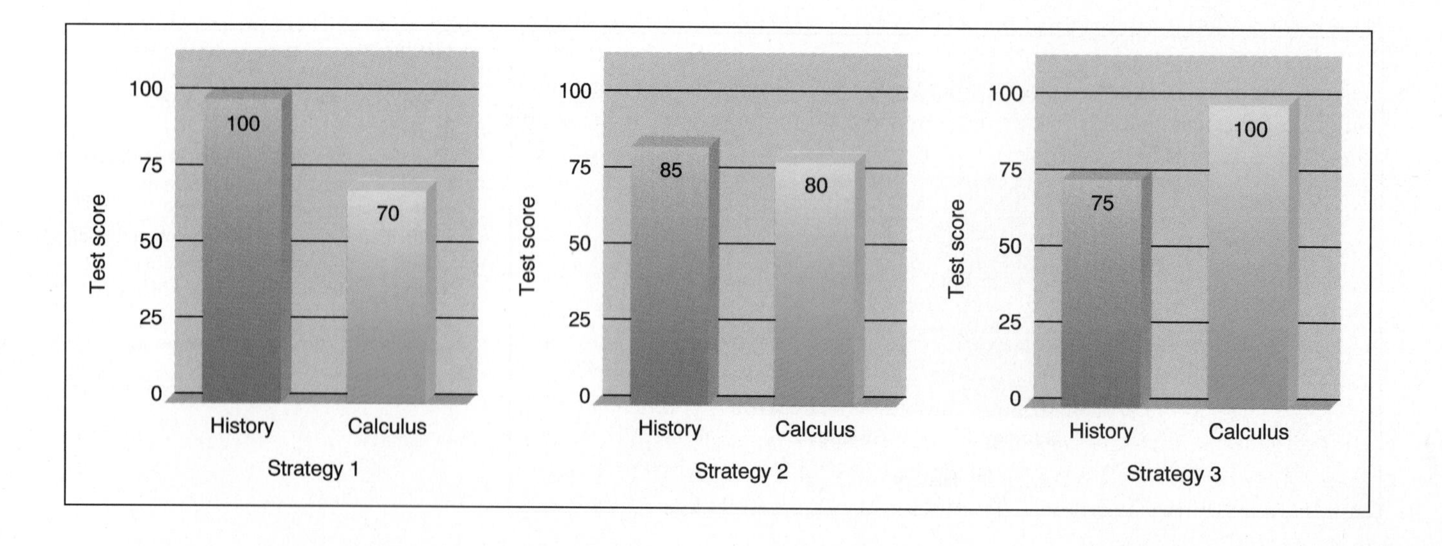

ber, getting 100 on both tests is impossible, given the structure of the economic problem. Assume for now that no other study strategy allows you to get above 70 on the calculus test, given that you get 100 on the history test. In this sense you have done as well as possible following this strategy. The third graph represents the opposite strategy, concentrating on calculus and letting history slide. This strategy allows you to get 100 on the calculus test and 75 on the history test. The second graph represents a more "balanced" strategy in that you allocate your studying time so you do fairly well on both tests. This strategy allows you to get 85 on the history test and 80 on the calculus test.

Which of these strategies best meets your objectives of getting 100 on both tests? The question has no answer without additional information on the relative worth you attach to the two subjects. All you do know is that both objectives are desirable and that you have insufficient time and knowledge to meet both of them. The notion of an efficient choice as one that best meets the objectives must be modified. Therefore, when there are two (or more) objectives, economists define **efficiency** as follows: An allocation (set of choices) is efficient if moving closer to any one objective is not possible without moving away from at least one other objective.

EFFICIENCY

A criterion for judging the solution to an economic problem that refers to making the choices that best meet the objectives; if the economic problem has a single objective, then efficiency means coming as close to the objective as possible; if the economic problem has more than one objective, then efficiency means that the Law of Substitution holds. A solution is efficient if moving closer to one objective requires moving farther away from at least one other objective.

To see what efficiency now implies, consider the strategy 2 in Figure 2.2, which gives you 85 on the history test and 80 on the calculus test. Suppose that you rethink your studying strategy and discover another strategy that would allow you to (1) increase your test score in history to 89, while maintaining your test score in calculus at 80; or (2) increase your test score in calculus to 84, while maintaining your test score in history at 85; or (3) increase both test scores, to 88 in history and 82 in calculus. The new study strategy is clearly better. Therefore, the original study strategy pictured in the middle graph of Figure 2.2 is shown to be inefficient—it does not best meet the objectives of getting 100 on both tests.

You may discover even better study strategies, but eventually such easy gains must end. At some point different study strategies will be able to increase one test score only at the expense of the other test score. You can do better on the history test only if you are willing to accept a lower score on the calculus test, or you can do better on the calculus test only if you are willing to accept a lower score on the history test. Whenever this situation occurs, a study strategy is efficient. The **Law of Substitution** holds: Moving closer to one objective can be achieved only by moving farther away from another objective. Efficiency, then, best meets multiple objectives in the narrow sense of achieving an absence of slack. In our example, slack means being able to score higher on one of the tests without reducing your score on the other test or being able to score higher on both tests.

LAW OF SUBSTITUTION

A test of efficiency with more than one objective that says that moving closer to one objective is possible only by moving farther away from at least one other objective.

LIMITATIONS OF THE EFFICIENCY CRITERION Finding efficient allocations is important because living with inefficient choices wastes scarce resources. When the economic problem has multiple objectives, however, the efficiency criterion is limited in the broader sense that it cannot solve the economic problem. It cannot determine the best allocation of resources. Return again to our study example and Figure 2.2. All three strategies pictured there could be efficient. Referring to the first graph, you may not be able to score above 70 in calculus without reducing your score in history below 100; the same may be true for the other strategies. Also, many other efficient study strategies may exist that produce combinations of test scores different from those pictured in the three graphs. If all these study strategies are efficient, which is best?

The efficiency criterion alone cannot answer this question. Study strategies in our example are either efficient or inefficient, and the efficiency criterion recognizes all efficient study strategies as equals. To reach a final solution requires an additional step. You must somehow assign a relative value, or weight, to your performance on each test and then judge which among all the efficient study strategies yields the highest weighted value of the two tests. The weighting scheme of relative values turns the two objectives into a single objective. For instance, you may be far more concerned with your history test score than with your calculus test score because history is your major. In that case you would place a relatively high weight on the history test score and a relatively low weight on the calculus test score. This, in turn, might lead you to prefer study strategy 1 in Figure 2.2 over the other two study strategies, even if all three study strategies are efficient. If, instead, you were concerned only with your overall grade point average, then you would give equal weight to both tests. In this case you would prefer the study strategy 3 in Figure 2.2 over the other two study strategies because its total score of 175 (175 = 100 + 75) exceeds the total scores of the other two study strategies (170 in the first graph and 165 in the second graph). Notice, though, that selecting a best strategy among a number of efficient strategies depends on whatever criterion you use to assign weights to the two test scores. You must be able to refine your objectives beyond the simple ideal of wanting to get 100 on both tests so that you turn the two objectives into a single objective, such as achieving the highest combined score.

## Equity

The limitation of the efficiency criterion is particularly distressing when analyzing broad social issues that are concerned with the economic well-being of individual citizens. Figure 2.3 provides an example. The bar graph in the figure illustrates the average income levels of two groups of people within a poor, primarily agricultural country such as Haiti. Group 1 consists of the landed aristocracy, a small minority of the population. They have an average annual income of $50,000 according to the figure, which allows them to enjoy a lavish lifestyle. Group 2 consists of the peasants who work the land, the vast majority of the population. Their average annual income is only $500 according to the figure, which allows them to achieve little more than a subsistence lifestyle, to purchase only the barest necessities of food, clothing, and shelter. Although the average income numbers in Figure 2.3 are hypothetical, they are representative of the huge disparity in income between the landed aristocracy and the peasant farmers in many poor countries.

Suppose that an economist could demonstrate that the economy of this country is efficient: The income of the peasants cannot be increased without decreasing the income of the aristocracy. The efficiency of the economy may not be a terribly compelling criterion in this instance. A number of people may well favor redistributing income from the aristocracy to the peasants, even if some inefficiencies arise in the process of redistributing. Such people are using an entirely different criterion for judging solutions to economic problems, one based on their sense of equity, or fairness.

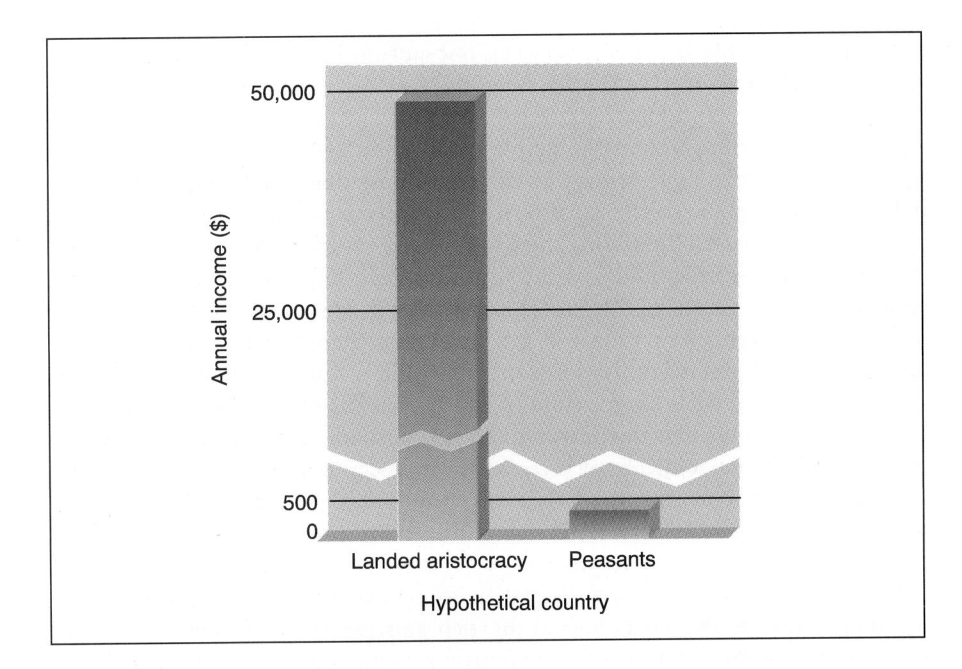


FIGURE 2.3

**Income Distribution in a Poor Agricultural Country (Hypothetical Data)**

The bar graphs show the distribution of income that is typical in poor agricultural countries. The landed aristocracy enjoy high incomes; the peasants who farm the land have meager incomes. The economy may be efficient. However, many people might not consider the distribution of income to be fair, and would be willing to redistribute income from the landed aristocracy to the peasant farmers.

The concern for equity in economic analysis expresses itself along two dimensions, equity in terms of economic outcomes or end results and equity in terms of the process that generated the end results. The end-results dimension of equity asks if the outcome is fair. Our hypothetical example in Figure 2.3 illustrates this concern. Should a small minority of the people be allowed to enjoy a lavish lifestyle while the vast majority of the people suffer a subsistence lifestyle? The process dimension of equity asks if the rules under which the economy operates are fair. Regardless of the outcome, did each individual in our hypothetical country have an equal chance of achieving a high standard of living?

END-RESULTS EQUITY The concern for **end-results equity,** or fair outcomes, is not limited to the poorer countries of the world. Even the richest countries have some people who enjoy very high incomes and other people who are desperately poor. Every society must decide if the government should redistribute income from the rich to the poor and, if so, how much income it should redistribute. The decision to redistribute income is never an easy one because the rich lose from a redistribution of income and the poor gain. This begs a very difficult question: How should society value the losses of the rich against the gains of the poor? Philosophers, theologians, natural and social scientists, people from all walks of life have wrestled for centuries with the issue of comparing the gains and losses of different people without arriving at a convincing answer. All we have are various suggestions based on highly personal interpretations of what constitutes a just distribution of resources.

END-RESULTS EQUITY

A criterion for judging the solution to an economic problem that asks whether economic outcomes are fair.

Economists tend to avoid the question altogether. According to economic Nobel laureate Wassily Leontief, economists agree on only two principles relating to end-results equity. The first principle is **consumer sovereignty:** Individuals are best able to judge their own self-interests. In particular, individuals can best determine how much they gain or lose in any given situation. The second principle is the efficiency principle applied to individuals: A policy

CONSUMER SOVEREIGNTY

The principle that individuals are best able to judge their own self-interests.

or event is desirable if it makes at least one person better off without making anyone else worse off. Neither principle is helpful in resolving the issue of comparing gainers and losers.[1]

The consumer sovereignty principle casts doubt on the ability to compare the gains and losses experienced by different individuals. Suppose that Bob is rich and Sue is poor, so the government proposes a redistributional policy of taxing Bob $100 and transferring the $100 to Sue. Can we really compare Bob's loss in utility or satisfaction from the tax *as determined by Bob himself* with Sue's gain of utility or satisfaction from the transfer *as determined by Sue herself?* They might not measure their utility in the same way. People's incomes are commonly used to measure utility in economic studies, but everyone realizes that income is a very inaccurate measure of utility. Worse yet, Bob (and others who are taxed) may overstate his losses to try to persuade the politicians to scrap the redistributional policy. Sue (and others who receive transfers) may overstate her gains to try to convince the politicians to adopt the policy. For these reasons most economists are skeptical of being able to compare gains and losses of different individuals *as the individuals themselves perceive them.*

Society may decide that a dollar taken from the rich and given to the poor has more value to the poor than to the rich and use this judgment as a basis for redistributing income. Most economists are uncomfortable with this justification, however, because the idea that additional dollars of income are more useful to the poor is based on personal value judgments, not scientific inquiry. No one can prove it is true. Also, the justification is imposed from outside; it does not honor the principle of consumer sovereignty. When a society decides to redistribute income, it is not necessarily weighing the losses and gains of the rich and the poor as the rich and the poor themselves perceive them. Nonetheless, many societies do justify their redistributional programs on the grounds that additional dollars of income are more useful to the poor.

The efficiency principle is especially compelling in a social context: Why not adopt a policy that makes some people better off without harming anyone else? But the efficiency principle is no help at all in resolving the fundamental question of end-results equity because it does not apply to situations involving gainers and losers. The efficiency principle cannot be used to compare Bob's losses with Sue's gains in the tax-transfer example. Moreover, we saw in the hypothetical example illustrated by Figure 2.3 that even the most extreme situation of wealth and poverty could be efficient. The efficiency criterion is satisfied whenever the Law of Substitution holds; that is, whenever giving more to one citizen will mean giving less to another. As such, it simply avoids all the difficult issues in society's quest for end-results equity.

The fundamental question of comparing gainers and losers arises in all social issues because economic events and government policies invariably benefit some people and harm others. A new superhighway from the city to the country benefits vacationers and all businesses that need to transport goods between city and country. At the same time it forces people who live along the route of the highway to relocate to other homes. Do the benefits of the vacationers and businesses outweigh losses of those who are forced to move? Also, does the answer to this question change depending on the incomes of the gainers and losers? Suppose that rich Bob is a vacationer who benefits from the highway and poor Sue is a homeowner who is forced to relocate. Alternatively,

---

[1] W. Leontief, *Essays in Economics: Theories and Theorizing* (New York: Oxford University Press, 1966), 27.

suppose poor Sue is the vacationer and rich Bob the homeowner. Should society feel the same about the gains and the losses in the two situations? No one has ever been able to resolve these difficult questions of end-results equity.

Perhaps the only consensus that has arisen in the area of end-results equity is the principle of **horizontal equity,** which requires that equals be treated equally. If two people are identical in every respect that is relevant to economic activity—if, for example, they have the same tastes, the same abilities, and the same desire to work hard—then they should achieve the same level of economic well-being. Horizontal equity is the economic equivalent of the legal principle that all people should be equal in the eyes of the law.

HORIZONTAL EQUITY
A principle of end-results equity that requires that equals receive equal treatment.

The principle of horizontal equity begs the question of whether two people are ever truly identical in every respect. Nonetheless, the principle is universally appealing because it rules out discrimination in economic affairs. Differences in economic well-being that are based on economically irrelevant characteristics such as sex, or race, or religious beliefs are inherently unfair. People should not be allowed to gain an economic advantage simply because they are male rather than female, white rather than black, or Protestant rather than Roman Catholic. Notice, though, that the principle of horizontal equity has nothing to say about how to treat unequals, for instance, the gifted versus the not-so-gifted. The treatment of unequals is the far tougher question in deciding whether economic outcomes are fair.

PROCESS EQUITY The concern for **process equity** in economic affairs is most closely associated today with the philosopher Robert Nozick. Nozick argues that any economic result is fair so long as the process generating the result is fair. Nozick's position has broad appeal, especially in the United States where the notion of fair play is a time-honored tradition. Americans hold dear the principle of **equality of opportunity**: Individuals should have equal access to whatever economic opportunities they are willing and able to pursue. This allows them to develop their economic potential to the fullest. Would most Americans go as far as Nozick and say that society should grant equal access to economic opportunities to all its members and let the chips fall where they may? Probably not, but a survey of U.S. business and political leaders by two professors at the Harvard Business School suggests that Americans do care more about process equity than end-results equity. The survey found that the business and political leaders are far more concerned about equality of opportunity than equality of results in economic affairs.[2]

PROCESS EQUITY
A criterion for judging economic activity that asks whether the rules under which the economy operates are fair.

EQUALITY OF OPPORTUNITY
A principle of process equity that requires that individuals have equal access to whatever economic opportunities they are willing and able to pursue so that they can develop their economic potential to the fullest.

When economists express a concern for equity in their professional writings, they are more likely to appeal to the process ideal of equality of opportunity than to any one ideal based on end-results equity. Equality of opportunity as a standard of equity will appear frequently throughout this text. Nonetheless, many economists would argue that end results matter, too. The most troubling aspect of Nozick's position is that the results of the economic game depend very much on the resources that people are able to bring to the game. Equal opportunity may not be enough. People lucky enough to be born with exceptional intelligence, or athletic ability, or competitive drive, or to have received a huge inheritance are far more likely to do well than are people without these advantages, no matter how the economic game is played. Society might be

[2]R. Nozick, "Distributive Justice," *Philosophy and Public Affairs* 3 (Spring 1973): 45–126; S. Verba, G. Orren, *Equality in America: the View from the Top* (Cambridge, MA: Harvard University Press, 1985), chapter 1.

quite willing to help people who fall behind because they were not so blessed from the start. Indeed, a society might be willing to help its poor simply because they are poor, whatever the reason.

REFLECTION: Do you think that by and large people are treated fairly in the U.S. economy? If not, do you believe that the problems lie with end-results or with process, or with both?

The twin goals of end-results equity and process equity are not entirely independent of one another. The process equity principle of equality of opportunity is closely linked to the end-results principle of horizontal equity. Identical people who have equal access to economic opportunities should be able to achieve the same level of economic well-being. In other words, equality of opportunity tends to produce horizontal equity. The inverse is also true. Equals do not usually reach the same level of economic well-being when they do not have equal access to economic opportunities, either because of outright discrimination or for some other reason. The link between equality of opportunity and horizontal equity is another theme that appears throughout this text.

## ECONOMISTS AS MODEL BUILDERS

Economists analyze social phenomena much as natural scientists analyze natural phenomena. When scientists study the natural environment, they often construct a portion of the environment in their laboratories so they can focus on the problem that interests them and conduct controlled experiments. A **controlled experiment** is a method of analysis that allows scientists to study the effects of changing one element in the environment at a time while holding all other elements in the environment constant. This is the way that scientists determine cause-and-effect relationships. If changing element A, but only element A, produces effect B, then A must cause B, since all other elements that might have caused B are being held constant in the controlled experiment and cannot influence B.

CONTROLLED EXPERIMENT

The scientific method of analysis for determining cause-and-effect relationships that studies the effects of changing one element in an environment at a time while holding constant all the other elements in the environment.

Economists believe that the controlled experiment is the proper way to study economic behavior. They operate under a handicap, however, because controlled experiments do not occur in society and economists cannot easily bring portions of society into a laboratory setting. Instead, they must confront economic events as they exist in the real world, and real-world environments are highly complex with many variables changing simultaneously. None of the conditions necessary for a controlled experiment are satisfied.

Economists respond to the complexities of actual events by *conceptualizing* a controlled experiment, even though they cannot actually conduct one. They construct a **model,** which is nothing more than a simplified description of some real-world situation. A model isolates one particular aspect of the situation so economists can study the effects on that one aspect as they change different elements of the model, one at a time. In other words, an economic model imitates the natural scientist's controlled experiment. Economic models can be expressed verbally, graphically, or mathematically. All three types of models will appear in this text, although the vast majority will be verbal or graphical.

MODEL

A simplified description of some real-world situation that isolates one particular aspect of the situation and studies the effects on that one aspect as different elements are changed one at a time.

Working with models takes some getting used to. Economic models have no intention of capturing every facet of reality, and this often bothers beginning students. Rather, the whole idea of building a model is to simplify, to capture the essence of a particular problem or event and take whatever insights come from the exercise. The test of a model is whether it tells us something useful about the real world.

A model can never describe all the complexities of the real world. Even if such a model existed, it would be as complicated as reality itself and utterly incomprehensible. No one claims to be able to understand human behavior and social interactions completely; this is why economists build models in the first place.

## Modeling the Studying Problem

Let's return to the problem of how best to study for final exams in order to see how economists use models to analyze economic problems. Determining the absolute best study strategy for your exams is clearly a difficult problem. It is hard enough just to know where to begin! You have many exams and, no doubt, much catching up to do. Time is limited, everyone is stressed out, and the campus is filled with annoying distractions. The studying problem during final exams is so difficult that no one can ever tell you exactly how you should study. Still, we have to think about the problem in some way.

The economist's approach is to simplify the problem. We will build a model of the studying problem that captures just a few of its essential elements and see what the model can tell us about how to study. In order to build a model, economists make a number of simplifying assumptions about the nature of the problem. Here we will make six assumptions about studying for exams that will simplify the studying problem as much as it can be. Taken together, these six assumptions constitute a model of the studying problem. Our model is so simple that we will be able to determine a best studying strategy.

Assume that

1. You have four two-hour exams next Monday at 8:00, 10:00, 12:00, and 2:00 in history, calculus, Russian, and astrology.
2. You figure that you will have 30 hours of time available for studying before the exams. Studying occurs in units of one hour each; studying a subject for less than an hour is useless.
3. If you do not study at all, you will receive a failing grade of 50 on each exam.
4. You know how much your score will improve in each subject for every hour spent studying the subject. The information is contained in Table 2.1. For instance, the first hour spent studying your easiest subject, astrology, improves your test score by 10 points, the second hour by 9 points more, the third hour by 7 points more, and so forth. The first hour spent studying Russian, your most difficult subject, will improve your test score by 4 points, the second hour by 3 points more, and so on.
5. Knowledge learned is never forgotten, and each subject is totally independent of the others. There is no extra gain in knowledge from spending a number of consecutive hours on one subject, and no loss in knowledge as you switch from subject to subject.
6. No matter how you decide to study, you cannot achieve 100 on all four exams. There is not enough time for that.

Your problem is to devise a studying strategy that assures you the highest total score on all four tests combined, in other words, the highest grade point average. What should you study during each of the 30 study units?

Before thinking about the proper strategy, be sure you can identify the objectives, alternatives, and constraints of this economic problem.

*Objective:* You want to achieve the highest total test score on all four subjects combined. (This study problem has a single objective, unlike the study problem described earlier in the chapter in which you cared about your performance on each of the tests.)

*Alternatives* (Choices): You must choose which subject to study in each of the 30 one-hour study units.

*Constraints:* Limited time and limited knowledge prevent you from scoring 100 on every test.

You have no doubt noticed that our model or description of the study problem assumes away a number of real-world complications. No one has to take four exams in one day. In real life, you may not be allowed to fail any of the exams, although you can in this problem. Knowledge learned is forgotten, so that switching your studying from subject to subject could be costly. No one knows exactly how much a test score will improve for each hour spent studying. The various stresses experienced during final exams are also ignored. Remember, an economic model captures the essence of a problem by simplifying it.

## The Margin in Economic Analysis

MARGIN

Refers to the effects of a small change in an economic variable.

What is the best studying strategy in this stylized situation? The key to the answer lies on the margin. The **margin** in economic analysis refers to the effects of a small change in an economic variable. In our study problem the only variable that can change is the amount of time spent studying a particular subject, and the smallest unit of time it can change is one hour. The improvement in the test score is the effect of changing the amount of studying by one hour. Therefore, each entry in Table 2.1 is defined as the marginal grade for a particular subject. The marginal grade indicates how much your test score changes (improves) for each additional hour of study.

The best studying strategy is easily stated in terms of marginal grades: *During every hour select the subject with the highest marginal grade.* That is, choose to study the subject each hour that yields the greatest improvement in the test score.

Apply the study strategy rule to the numbers in Table 2.1. You should spend the first hour studying astrology. Its 10-point improvement exceeds that for any other subject. The second hour should also be spent on astrology because the 9-point improvement is the best you can do that hour. Switch to calculus in the third hour to pick up 8 points. In the fourth and fifty hours study history and astrology in either order. You gain 7 points for studying either subject during those hours. Next, switch to calculus in the sixth hour to earn an ad-

**TABLE 2.1 Improvement in Test Scores for Each Additional Hour of Study**

| HOUR | HISTORY | CALCULUS | RUSSIAN | ASTROLOGY |
|---|---|---|---|---|
| 1st | 7 | 8 | 4 | 10 |
| 2nd | 5 | 6 | 3 | 9 |
| 3rd | 5 | 4 | 3 | 7 |
| 4th | 5 | 4 | 2 | 5 |
| 5th | 4 | 4 | 2 | 5 |
| 6th | 3 | 4 | 2 | 4 |
| 7th | 3 | 3 | 1 | 3 |
| 8th | 3 | 3 | 1 | 3 |
| 9th | 2 | 2 | 1 | 2 |
| 10th | 2 | 2 | 1 | 2 |

ditional 6 points. Continuing in this manner until the 30 hours are exhausted guarantees you the highest total score. You do not even have to keep track of your total score. To allocate your scarce time efficiently simply ask: What is true on the margin? Then select the highest marginal grade each time.

What is true on the margin is the single most important issue in economic analysis. It will appear time and again in our study of economics. Looking at the margin is the essence of all controlled scientific experiments because these experiments are specifically designed to study the effects of making small changes in a variable. Since economic models are conceptualized controlled experiments, the margin is central to economic analysis as well. In particular, our study problem shows that the key to solving the economic problem lies in the margin. We will see that nearly all efficient strategies for allocating scarce resources are described by rules involving the margin that are as simple as our studying rule.

### Does the Model Pass the Test?

Our model of studying for exams is simple enough to yield a precise and simple studying strategy. Now let's put our model to the test. Does this admittedly simplified model tell us anything useful about the real-life problem of studying? Yes, it does. It yields an important insight that applies both to studying for exams and to taking exams: Do not waste precious time spinning your wheels on subjects or problems that are overly difficult. Study your easier subjects first because that will improve your overall grade point average the most. In our problem, spending hour upon hour trying to learn Russian is exactly the wrong thing to do. Our model suggests that when taking exams, you should always begin with the questions you know best. Earn points right away, rather than staring blankly at a difficult question for most of the exam period. (Starting with what you know has the additional advantage of relaxing you.)

The studying problem becomes more complicated if you cannot fail any one subject (or any one question on a test). You may have to spend much of your time on more difficult material in this case. But then our model highlights something you already know. The stricture against failing a subject has a very high opportunity cost in terms of your grade point average because it drags down other subjects as well. This is one reason why students drop subjects they are in danger of failing. Our simplified model tells us quite a bit about the student's economic problem after all. It passes the test of being a good model.

REFLECTION: How do you go about studying for a number of final exams? What assumptions about the economic problem of studying for exams lie behind your studying strategy?

## NORMATIVE AND POSITIVE ANALYSIS

Economic analysis is traditionally divided into normative analysis and positive analysis. **Normative economic analysis** is the study of what *ought to be.* It attempts to determine appropriate norms or criteria for judging the results of economic behavior and activity. Normative statements cannot be shown to be true or false by testing them against real-world data and behavior. Instead, they rely on fundamental value judgments that people may choose to accept or reject. They are not subject to proof. **Positive economic analysis** refers to the study of what *is.* It attempts to determine what actually exists out there in the real world. All positive statements are testable. In principle, real-world data

NORMATIVE ECONOMIC ANALYSIS
The study of what ought to be; attempts to determine appropriate norms or criteria for judging the results of economic behavior and activity.

POSITIVE ECONOMIC ANALYSIS
The study of what is; attempts to determine what actually exists in the real world and to describe the consequences of economic decisions.

can prove whether a positive statement is true or false. Both normative analysis and positive analysis have important roles to play in the two broad subject areas of economics, the study of the economic problem and the study of exchange.

## Analyzing the Economic Problem

Regarding the economic problem, the first task falls upon normative analysis to describe the objectives on the basis of individual or social norms. What are the goals to be achieved, and why? Once normative analysis has described the objectives, positive analysis then determines the alternatives and the constraints of the problem and describes the effects of various choices on both the objectives and the constraints. Normative analysis reappears to judge the solution to the economic problem on the basis of efficiency and equity. Is the solution efficient? And, in some contexts, is the solution equitable? The following example illustrates the interplay of normative analysis and positive analysis in solving an economic problem.

Suppose that the officials of a local community decide that they want to improve the academic quality of the high school. They believe that a better high school education will give the town's children better job opportunities and allow them to lead more cultured and examined lives. The normative basis of their decision is the value judgment that economic well-being, culture, and living the examined life are all worthwhile objectives. The choice to pursue these objectives by improving the high school is one of the alternatives and the beginning of the positive analysis of the problem. There are other ways to achieve these objectives, but the officials made this choice based on their own experiences and on studies about the actual relationship between a high school education and the objectives.

Positive analysis has more to add about the alternatives and the constraints. What are the choices for improving the quality of the high school? The officials can recruit more, and better, teachers; increase the length of the school day, or school year; de-emphasize the nonacademic parts of the curriculum; improve classroom facilities; and use more computerized instruction. What are the constraints: Is the budget for the high school set, or might it be increased by raising taxes, or applying for state or federal aid, or reducing other areas of the town's budget?

Positive analysis is also needed to determine the effect of the various alternatives on both the objectives and the constraints. What do we know about the effectiveness of the various options for improving quality? Do better teachers, longer school days, better facilities, and smaller class sizes really improve the quality of education? What does each of these options cost? How much must salaries rise to attract better teachers? And so forth.

Once positive analysis has described the structure of the problem, normative analysis judges whether the officials have achieved an efficient solution to their problem. Have they achieved the maximum improvement in educational quality, given the resources available to them? If not, what different choices would improve quality more for the same costs? The efficient solution depends on the effectiveness of the various options in improving educational quality and on their respective costs. Equity may also be an issue. Suppose that one set of choices lets the brightest students reach their full academic potential, but leaves the average students behind. Another set of choices improves the education of all students to some extent, but leaves the brightest students far short of achieving their full academic potential. The town will have to appeal to its sense of what is fair to determine which set of choices is better (assuming they cost the same).

### Analyzing Economic Exchange

Regarding economic exchange, normative analysis establishes the norms for judging the effectiveness of economic exchanges. Economists judge economic exchanges using the norms of efficiency and equity, the same norms used to judge the solutions to economic problems.

The positive analysis of exchange describes the actual conditions under which exchange takes place and determines the implications of those conditions. Exchange occurs in a number of different environments. Wheat is produced by thousands of farmers and turned into a wide variety of products that reach hundreds of millions of consumers each day. The consumers and farmers never actually meet. Airplanes, in contrast, are produced by a handful of business firms and sold to a small number of other firms and to governments. The buyers and sellers are in close contact with each other. What results can be expected in each of these environments? What will the prices be? The quantities exchanged? Will the exchanges be orderly? The norms of efficiency and equity complete the analysis. Will the exchanges generate an efficient allocation of resources? Will they be even-handed and fair to all parties.

Positive analysis also describes how economic exchanges respond to government policy initiatives. How will individuals and business firms react to a 1 percent increase in a state's sales tax? If the federal government adds $5 billion to its educational grant-in-aid programs for state and local governments, will state and local spending for education increase by $5 billion? By more than $5 billion? By less than $5 billion? Positive analysis of this kind is obviously central to the conduct of effective government policy. The best of intentions can easily go awry if governments misjudge the responses to their policies.

## MICROECONOMICS AND MACROECONOMICS

The study of economics is traditionally divided into microeconomics and macroeconomics. This text follows that tradition.

### Microeconomics

As the name suggests, **microeconomics** studies the economy "in the small." Microeconomics takes snapshots of tiny sections of the economy and magnifies them. It focuses on (1) the economic problems of individual consumers, business firms, and government agencies; (2) the incentives that motivate them to engage in economic exchanges with one another; and (3) the results of their economic exchanges for particular products and factors of production, such as automobiles or labor. The vast majority of economic exchanges take place in

MICROECONOMICS
The study of the economy "in the small"; analyzes the economic problems of individual economic agents and the exchanges between them.

organized markets in the U.S. economy. Therefore, our study of microeconomics will concentrate on how markets work in the United States.

Microeconomics attempts to answer the following kinds of questions: Why do markets form so easily? What causes the prices of individual products to rise and fall? Should the government give poor families food stamps as well as cash? Is good weather necessarily good for farmers? Does minimum wage legislation prevent teen-agers from finding jobs? Why do 30 million Americans live in poverty? How do large corporations use their market power to increase their profits? To what extent does discrimination explain the fact that women receive lower wages than men? Are U.S. markets generally efficient or inefficient? Will the job prospects of college graduates improve over the next five years? Do taxes destroy people's incentives to work?

You will be better able to answer these questions when you have completed the microeconomic chapters.

## Macroeconomics

MACROECONOMICS
The study of the economy "in the large"; analyzes the overall performance of the economy.

FULL EMPLOYMENT
The condition when all people who want to work have a job.

UNEMPLOYMENT
The condition when people are actively looking for work, but are unable to find a suitable job.

PRICE STABILITY
Prices in general are neither rising nor falling.

PRICE INFLATION
A persistent increase in the prices of most goods and services.

LONG-RUN ECONOMIC GROWTH
A continuing process in which the economy is able to produce ever-increasing amounts of goods and services year after year.

STABLE DOLLAR
The value of the dollar remains constant relative to the currencies of other nations.

**Macroeconomics** studies the economy "in the large," that is, the overall performance of the economy. It focuses on aggregate data such as the total consumption by all consumers, the total investment in plant and equipment by all business firms, the combined spending of all government agencies, the entirety of U.S. economic interactions with the other nations of the world, the total employment in all labor markets, and the total income earned and output produced by all factors of production.

Economists judge the overall performance of an economy on the basis of four broad objectives called the macroeconomic policy goals: full employment, price stability, long-run economic growth, and stability in a nation's international economic relations.

- **Full employment** exists whenever there is a job for all people who want to work. **Unemployment** exists whenever people are actively looking for work, but are unable to find a suitable job.
- **Price stability** occurs whenever prices in general are neither rising nor falling. Most nations today wrestle with the problem of **price inflation,** which is a persistent increase in the prices of most goods and services.
- **Long-run economic growth** is taking place whenever the economy is able to produce ever-increasing amounts of goods and services year after year.
- **Stability in international economic relations** has two dimensions. One is achieving an equality between the value of the nation's imports from other countries and the value of its exports to other countries. The other is achieving a stable dollar. A **stable dollar** exists whenever the value of the dollar remains constant relative to the currencies of other nations, such as the Japanese yen or French franc.

Pursuing the first three macroeconomic policy goals is a matter or law in the United States. Both the Employment Act of 1946 and the Humphrey-Hawkins Act of 1978 require the federal government to formulate economic policies that promote maximum employment, production (growth), and purchasing power (stable prices). No U.S. laws require an equality between imports and exports or a stable dollar, but even the most casual observer of economic events knows that the United States is deeply concerned about each of these issues.

The United States does not usually attempt to achieve the macroeconomic policy goals directly. National, state, and local governments do not routinely employ all the unemployed. Governments directly control only a very few prices. No government can dictate the rate of economic growth. The federal government does place some direct controls on international trade and makes some attempts to influence the value of the dollar, but by and large trade is free, and the value of the dollar is set in the marketplace. The federal government's macroeconomic policies are directed instead toward the overall level of economic activity. The idea is to try to achieve the macroeconomic policy goals indirectly by influencing the performance of the entire economy.

The macroeconomic policy record over the past twenty years has not been especially impressive. Unemployment averaged 6.1 percent of the labor force in the 1970s, 7.2 percent in the 1980s, and 6.5 percent in the first three years of the 1990s. These percentages are higher than the American public, and many economists, are willing to accept. Prices have not been stable. They rose an average of 7.1 percent per year in the 1970s, 5.6 percent per year in the 1980s, and 4.1 percent in the first three years of the 1990s. Since 1973 the rate of economic growth has been far below its trend for the entire twentieth century. The United States has not been able to achieve equality between its imports and exports. The value of imports has greatly exceeded the value of exports since 1981. Finally, the dollar has been very unstable. The value of the dollar fell steadily relative to most foreign currencies throughout most of the 1970s, rose sharply in the early and mid-1980s, and then fell again in the late 1980s and into the 1990s.

REFLECTION: Which of the four macroeconomic policy goals does the Clinton administration seem to be most concerned about? The least concerned about?

The macroeconomic chapters will explain how the government's macroeconomic policies attempt to achieve the macroeconomic policy goals and why they often do not succeed.

## SUMMARY

The first section of Chapter 2 discussed the two criteria that economists use to judge the solutions to economic problems, efficiency and equity.

1. The meaning of efficiency depends on whether the economic problem has one or more objectives.
   a. If the economic problem has a single objective, then efficiency means coming as close to the objective as possible. If the objective has no natural limit, then efficiency means maximizing the objective. For example, a firm is efficient if it is maximizing its profit.
   b. If the economic problem has more than one objective, then efficiency means that the Law of Substitution holds: A solution is efficient if moving closer to one objective requires moving farther away from at least one other objective.
2. Equity has two dimensions, end-results equity and process equity. End-results equity judges whether economic outcomes are fair. Process equity judges whether the rules under which the economy operates are fair.
3. Economic events and policies invariably help some people and harm others. The fundamental question of end-results equity is how to evaluate and compare the benefits of those who gain against the losses of those who lose. The only consensus that has emerged on this question is the principle

of horizontal equity: equal treatment of equals. When horizontal equity exists, two individuals who are identical in every relevant economic aspect achieve the same level of utility or satisfaction.

4. A widely embraced principle of process equity is equality of opportunity, that people should have equal access to whatever economic opportunities they are willing and able to pursue.
5. Process equity and end-results equity are linked by the principles of equality of opportunity and horizontal equity because equality of opportunity tends to produce horizontal equity.

The second section of the chapter described the use of models in economic analysis.

6. A model is a simplified description of reality that tries to capture the essential features of real-world issues and events. Economic models are conceptual versions of the natural scientist's controlled laboratory experiment. Like controlled experiments, economic models are useful for discovering cause-and-effect relationships because they allow the economist to study the effects of changing one economic variable while holding all other variables constant.
7. Economists always ask: What is true on the margin? The margin refers to the effects of small changes in an economic variable. Looking at the margin is important because it points the way to efficient solutions of the economic problem.

The third section of the chapter described the distinction between normative and positive economic analysis.

8. Normative analysis studies what ought to be. It develops the norms or criteria for judging the solutions to economic problems and the results of economic exchanges. The two norms in economic analysis are efficiency and equity. Normative analysis also determines the objectives of an economic problem. All normative statements are based on value judgments; they cannot be proved or disproved.
9. Positive analysis studies what is. It describes the alternatives and constraints of the economic problem and indicates how the alternatives relate to both the objectives and the constraints. Positive analysis also describes how the conditions under which economic exchanges take place determine the results of the exchanges. Positive statements can be tested with real-world data; in principle, they can be shown to be true or false.

The final section of Chapter 2 discussed the distinction between microeconomics and macroeconomics.

10. Microeconomics studies the economy "in the small." It focuses on the economic problems of individual consumers, business firms, and government agencies; the incentives that motivate them to engage in economic exchanges with one another, and the results of their economic exchanges for particular products and factors of production.
11. Macroeconomics studies the economy "in the large." It focuses on the overall level of economic activity. Economists use four objectives to judge the performance of an economy: full employment, price stability, long-run economic growth, and stability in a nation's international economic relations.